JOINING AL-QAEDA

Jihadist Recruitment in Europe

PETER R. NEUMANN

ADELPHI PAPER 399

The International Institute for Strategic Studies

Arundel House | 13–15 Arundel Street | Temple Place | London | WC2R 3DX | UK

ADELPHI PAPER 399

First published December 2008 by **Routledge**
4 Park Square, Milton Park, Abingdon, Oxon, OX14 4RN

for **The International Institute for Strategic Studies**
Arundel House, 13–15 Arundel Street, Temple Place, London, WC2R 3DX, UK
www.iiss.org

Simultaneously published in the USA and Canada by **Routledge**
270 Madison Ave., New York, NY 10016

Routledge is an imprint of Taylor & Francis, an Informa Business

DIRECTOR-GENERAL AND CHIEF EXECUTIVE John Chipman
EDITOR Tim Huxley
EDITORIAL Ayse Abdullah, Katharine Fletcher
COPY EDITOR Jill Dobson
PRODUCTION John Buck
COVER IMAGE Stefan Rousseau/PA

Printed and bound in Great Britain by Bell & Bain Ltd, Thornliebank, Glasgow

British Library Cataloguing in Publication Data
A catalogue record for this book is available from the British Library

Library of Congress Cataloging in Publication Data
A catalogue record for this book is available from the Library of Congress

ISBN 978-0-415-54731-4
ISSN 0567-932X

Contents

INTRODUCTION

In late November 2006, Eliza Manningham-Buller, the director general of the British Security Service – more commonly known as MI5 – gave a public speech in which she warned of the continuing threat from 'home-grown' terrorism. She said that her service knew of 1,600 individuals in the United Kingdom who were part of Islamist militant structures.[1] Almost exactly one year later, Manningham-Buller's successor, Jonathan Evans, updated the figures, announcing that the number had risen to 2,000, with perhaps another 2,000 whose identities were unknown to MI5.[2] What neither of the two directors general told their audience was how these structures had arisen and how they had come to be populated with such significant numbers of people.

The question of how individuals move from political extremism to being actively engaged in violent and/or terrorist groups is one of the least understood issues in the debate about terrorism and counter-terrorism. Hundreds of scholarly papers have attempted to explain people's drift into political extremism (that is, their radicalisation), but little is known about the ways in which – once radicalised – individuals become members of groups that support and/or engage in violence. There are dozens of theories concerning what causes radicalisation, but there is no fully developed theory of terrorist recruitment, nor has there been any attempt to develop a conceptual framework examining the issue more systematically.

In the absence of a coherent body of serious analytical work, crude ideas and muddled thinking continue to hold sway. Yet, if recruitment is to be countered, it first needs to be understood. This paper aims to promote understanding of recruitment into the Islamist militant movement in Western Europe. It explores the nature of the process whereby individuals join the Islamist militant movement, and highlights relevant conditions, trends and developments that are believed to have a significant impact on the recruitment trajectory. Based on a comprehensive and up-to-date overview of the phenomenon, it then suggests how a series of recommendations through which recruitment into violent extremism might be curbed. While some of the findings may be applicable to other places and extremist movements, many are unique to Western Europe, and this should be kept in mind. In fact, as will be shown in Chapter 1, even within Western Europe, the conditions that facilitate recruitment differ substantially from country to country. The paper is based – to a large extent – on the author's final report for a research project funded by the European Commission (EC).[3] A substantial part of the field work was carried out by a team of collaborators – especially Luiz Martinez at Sciences Po in Paris, Rogelio Alonso at the University King Juan Carlos in Madrid, and Brooke Rogers at King's College London – whose contributions will be acknowledged where appropriate. Needless to say, the analysis and the conclusions that are contained in this paper reflect the author's views, not those of the European Commission or any of the collaborators who participated in the research.

Chapter 1 outlines some of the underlying conditions, structures and dynamics for radicalisation and recruitment in Western Europe. In Chapter 2, the paper examines whether particular places – often referred to as 'recruitment grounds' – are significant in terrorist recruitment. Chapter 3 concentrates on the 'recruiters'. In Chapter 4, the paper looks at the messages used at the various stages of recruitment. Chapter 5 focuses on the Internet as a new environment in which radicalisation and recruitment take place. The conclusion sets out some recommendations which follow from the analysis provided in the main part of the paper and may help policymakers in thinking about possible counter-strategies.

Concepts and terminology

What is recruitment, and how does it relate to radicalisation? Although the two terms denote distinct phenomena, they are often used in conjunction and little effort is made to distinguish between them. Radicalisation is about the change in attitude that may lead individuals to embrace extra-constitutional methods of bringing about political change, including – ultimately – the use of violence.[4] Recruitment, on the other hand, describes the process of joining a violent group. Conceptually, therefore, one may think of recruitment as being the link between radicalisation and the active pursuit of violence. In the words of the Danish researcher Michael Taarnby, it represents 'the bridge between personal belief and violent activism'.[5]

In practice, of course, it is neither useful nor feasible to view the two concepts separately. Many elements of the recruitment process cannot be understood without reflecting on individuals' pathways into radicalisation. Hence, whilst keeping in mind that radicalisation and recruitment can be thought of as entirely separate, it will be necessary to adopt a second, broader frame that contextualises the 'process of joining a violent group'. Recruitment – alongside 'grievance' and 'ideology' – constitutes one of the three elements around which most of the existing models of radicalisation revolve.[6] Without grievances – real or perceived – radical ideologies will not resonate. Without ideology, grievances may lead to crime and other forms of disorder and delinquency but are unlikely to result in politically motivated violence. And without recruitment, it will be impossible to channel individuals' sense of political frustration into collective action.[7] Indeed, it is the interplay between mobilisation, grievances and ideology that is critical to understanding how processes of recruitment unfold.

How, then, should recruitment be defined? In the popular understanding, the process of recruitment is a 'top-down' activity led by an organisation that seeks to attract new members. Even some of the more recent studies of terrorist recruitment reflect this interpretation. In a 2002 report, for example, the Dutch domestic intelligence service defined recruitment as the process whereby individuals are 'spotted … monitored … and manipulated … with the final purpose of having these people participate in the jihad'.[8] However, many analysts of contemporary jihadist recruitment believe that 'top-down' recruitment represents just one side of the coin. The American psychologist Marc Sageman, for instance, has argued that joining the Islamist militant movement is 'more of a bottom-up than a top-down activity' in which individuals are actively seeking out opportunities rather than being 'tricked', 'manipulated' or 'brainwashed' into becoming members.[9] For Sageman, al-Qaeda is akin to a elite university, which – rather than having to advertise – can sit back, wait for applicants to knock on its doors, and then pick the ones who are most suitable.[10] Whether Islamist militant recruitment in Europe is top-down or bottom-up is one of the questions this paper hopes to investigate. It will be important, therefore, to keep an open mind and define recruitment in the broadest possible terms, that is, as *the process through which individuals join entities engaged in violent extremism.*

Another term used throughout this paper is 'extremism'. The term can be used to refer to the *political ideologies* that are opposed to a society's core values and principles, which – in the context of European liberal democracies – could be said of any ideology that advocates racial or religious supremacy and/or opposes the core principles of democracy and human dignity.[11] The expression can also be used to describe the *methods* through which political actors attempt to realise their aims, that is, by using means that 'show disregard for the life, liberty, and human rights of others'.[12] In the absence of a consensus, it makes sense to qualify the concept – where necessary – by adding the appropriate adjective, that is, 'violent extremism' or 'ideological extremism'.

The type of violence which this paper is mostly concerned with is terrorism. Terrorism, of course, may well be the most contested word in the contemporary political vocabulary.[13] There is no agreed definition of terrorism in international law, nor is there any agreement amongst scholars. In the late 1980s, two researchers, Alex Schmid and Albert Jongman, conducted an extensive survey amongst leading academics in the field, concluding that its 'violent' nature was the only characteristic of terrorism which nearly everyone could agree upon.[14] In order to avoid the seemingly never-ending debate about the definition of terrorism, this paper follows the proposal put forward by the United Nations' High-Level Panel on Threat, Challenges and Changes, which – in its 2004 report – defined terrorism as '*any action… that is intended to cause death or serious bodily harm to civilians or non-combatants,* when the purpose of such an act … is to intimidate a population, or to compel a Government or an international organization to do or to abstain from doing any act' (emphasis added).[15] This definition is by no means perfect, but – for the purposes of this paper, which focuses not primarily on the violent manifestations of terrorism but rather the structures that are used to facilitate it – it seems acceptable.

Finally, what is meant by 'Islamist militancy'? Any observer of the debate about terrorism and counter-terrorism in the post-11 September 2001 era will know that it is nearly impossible to describe the movement that has been responsible for the terrorist attacks in Washington and New York as well as those in Madrid and London with accuracy and without causing offence by joining together Islam and terrorism and/or militancy.[16] Much of the relevant literature suggests that what all the perpetrators involved in these attacks share is a strict, literalist practice of Sunni Islam (frequently referred to as Wahhabism or Salafism),[17] a political agenda (Islamism) that – in its widest-ranging expression – proclaims that a worldwide community of believers (the *umma*) should be united or liberated under

Islamic rule, and the idea that the principal way of achieving this goal is through 'armed struggle' (jihad). (Needless to say, the concept of jihad has a variety of meanings in Islamic theology, but Islamist militants use it almost exclusively in the context of armed struggle.)[18] The expression 'Islamist militancy' may thus be a fairly accurate description of the kind of ideology which has been embraced by the movement that is the subject of this study. Others may simply want to refer to it as al-Qaeda, though – as will be seen in Chapter 1 – doing so raises as many questions as it answers.

Note on methodology

Before delving into the substance, it may be useful to comment briefly on how this study was carried out. The research was carried out mostly in 2007, and the final report was released in October 2008.[19] In part, the research involved extensively reviewing the literature related to recruitment, radicalisation and violent extremism. The project also evaluated policy reports by governments and independent researchers, and other publicly available materials, including news reports.

However, the most important and original part of the research derived from nearly 40 semi-structured interviews with individuals in France, Spain and the United Kingdom. Interviewees were drawn from three target populations: law-enforcement and intelligence officials who were dealing with violent extremism and radicalisation; community leaders such as imams and youth workers with experience of extremist recruitment; and radicals and former radicals who were members of, or close to, networks that approved of or facilitated violent extremism.

This multi-tiered approach made it possible to look at recruitment from various angles. Law-enforcement officers provided a bird's-eye perspective of the phenomenon and could compare different manifestations of recruitment over a wider geographical area. Community leaders offered insights into how organised networks and groups were making their presence felt in one particular community. Radicals and former radicals were in a good position to talk about the subjective experience of being recruited or wanting to join an extremist movement. All of them were granted anonymity, though their nationality and other non-attributable background information is specified where necessary.

The interviews do not constitute a representative sample, but – together with the other source materials and the existing secondary literature – it was possible to form a picture of recruitment for the Islamist militant movement in Europe. Though most of the primary source evidence used in this paper relates to developments in France, Spain and the United Kingdom, three countries where about half of the Muslim population in Western Europe resides,[20] the study also looked at other countries in Western Europe. The totality of available sources made it possible to discern similarities and differences in the patterns, structures and processes that form part of, and relate to, Islamist militant recruitment in Western Europe.

CHAPTER ONE

Dynamics and Structures

More than seven years after the 11 September 2001 attacks, much media reporting about al-Qaeda still presents the Islamist militant movement as a monolithic organisation, with similar structures and modes of conduct wherever it operates.[1] In consequence, it is often assumed that the pathways into Islamist militancy – the methods and means through which people radicalise and enter the movement – are uniform across the globe. Nothing could be further from the truth.

As will be shown in this chapter, there is considerable complexity in the process that underlies radicalisation and recruitment. Radicalisation and recruitment into the Islamist militant movement in Europe differ from similar processes in the Middle East or South Asia, and there are significant differences between Muslim communities within Europe. Moreover, the structures into which individuals are recruited are neither cohesive nor static, but – rather – reflect the amorphous nature of the movement as a whole. What emerges, therefore, is a highly dynamic picture, proving that an assessment of recruitment into the Islamist militant movement can never provide more than a snapshot that constantly needs to be updated and tested against reality.

Pathways into radicalisation

In recent years, it has become fashionable among analysts and commentators[2] to speak about 'European Muslims' as if they represent one unified group with similar ethnic, cultural and socio-economic characteristics. Yet the available demographic data on European Muslims reveals that they are divided among numerous communities. Estimates of the number of Muslims in Europe vary, given that some countries – including, most notably, France – do not record religious affiliation in their censuses. The figure of 20 million is widely accepted, though this includes at least seven million Muslims (some belonging to majority communities) in Eastern Europe and the Balkans who will not be considered here. The remaining 13m, who are spread across Western Europe, have little in common beyond adhering to the same faith (which, itself, is split into various sects) and the fact that they are minority, immigrant populations whose social and economic status is below national averages.[3]

If Muslim faith, minority status and economic disadvantage were sufficient explanations for al-Qaeda-inspired radicalisation and recruitment, one would expect the structures and dynamics of Islamist militancy to be uniform across Western Europe. They are not, of course: important variables have shaped and influenced the structures of the Islamist militant movement in Europe.

The first variable is the history of immigration. One of the most prominent explanations for radicalisation in Europe – put forward by the French political scientist Olivier Roy and others – is that the second- or third-generation descendants of Muslim immigrants are experiencing a powerful conflict of identity that makes them susceptible to Islamist militant ideology. Thus young Muslims are torn between the traditional culture of their parents and grandparents, which – in many respects – no longer makes any sense in the context of late modern, industrialised societies, and the cultures of Western societies, which – though superficially open and attractive – still regard them as foreigners and make it hard for them to integrate. As a consequence, many young Muslims have become open to the idea of joining a global, albeit virtual community of believers – the *umma* – which transcends national boundaries and is superior to identities derived from ethnicity or nationality. Indeed, as Roy points out, adopting this transnational frame allows them to rebel both against their parents and Western society at the same time.[4]

Evidence for this can be found in those Western European countries where the initial wave of Muslim immigration occurred during the post-war economic boom, with the first generation of predominantly male guest workers settling in the 1950s and 1960s and their wives and extended families following them in the 1970s. This is what happened in countries like Britain, France and Germany, where the second and (in some cases) third generation are now adults. However, the theory fails to make sense in countries such as Italy and Spain, which became destinations for immigration only later. The case of Spain is particularly striking: whereas before 1990, the entire Muslim population consisted of just 2,500 people, the number had increased to more than half a million by the early 2000s and continues to rise.[5] In Italy as well, the majority of the Muslim population was born outside Europe, and the process of radicalisation consequently follows a different trajectory from that seen in Britain, France and Germany.

European Muslim communities also differ in terms of their countries or regions of origin. While Turks settled in Germany, North Africans went to France, and later Italy and Spain. South Asian Muslims went largely to Britain. The Netherlands is unique in having received Muslim immigrants from all these backgrounds. Scandinavian countries, in addition to being a destination for immigrants from Turkey and South Asia, have seen significant inflows from the Middle East and East Africa. It would be wrong, therefore, to think of 'European Muslims' as being rooted in a particular culture or having a distinct ethnic profile.[6]

These differences matter, because Islamist militant radicalisation and recruitment have, at times, been related to particular regional conflicts outside Europe. The most obvious example is the Algerian civil war in the 1990s, which led to terrorist attacks in France but had no immediate consequences for most other European countries. Another instance of regional 'spillover' is the conflict in Kashmir, which became a focal point for the Muslim community in Britain, but was of lesser importance to Muslim communities in continental Europe.[7] Indeed, according to British security sources, the reason why Britain continues to be the 'centre of gravity' for the Islamist militant movement in Europe is precisely because of the historical links between the British Muslim community and Pakistan, with the result that recent instability there has been imported into Europe via the United Kingdom.[8]

More generally, diverse ethnic and national backgrounds have resulted in Muslim communities with vastly different attitudes towards a range of cultural and social issues. In opinion polls, for example, Muslim support for the introduction of sharia law is highly uneven across European countries, ranging from a significant minority among British Muslims to negligible among German Muslims.[9] These differences cannot be explained by Muslims' experience in Europe alone, but must be seen in the context of the cultures in which they were brought up. Most German Muslims' families originated in Turkey, where the separation between state and religious law was settled more than 80 years ago; nearly half of all British Muslims have roots in Pakistan,[10] where the sharia continues to be a strong source of legislation as well as national identity.

Another significant variable involves the diverse languages spoken by European Muslim communities. This difference cuts across generations and countries. For example, in contrast to their co-religionists in Britain and Germany, Muslims in France, Italy and Spain can use Arabic language writings and media, because most of their communities are rooted in Arabic-speaking North Africa. Second- and third-generation European Muslims, wherever they live, prefer European languages as their primary means of communication.

This may not seem hugely relevant at first, but it has profound consequences for the ways in which European Muslims are radicalised and recruited into the Islamist militant movement. For example, the success of a radical preacher like Abu Hamza in appealing to young Muslims of Pakistani descent can be explained, at least in part, by the fact that he was able to communicate with his (second- and third-generation) audience in English at a time when most of the services and prayers at mosques in Britain were still held in Urdu. Being Egyptian, he also spoke fluent Arabic, with the result that his followers regarded him as an authority on the Koran, even though he had had no theological training.

Another variable arises from the fact that Western European Muslims live in different countries, and that each national community experiences different national policies on immigration, integration, accommodation of faith practices, and foreign affairs. The connection between government policies and radicalisation can be straightforward. There can be no question, for example, that the invasion of Iraq contributed significantly to domestic radicalisation and recruitment in countries like Britain, which actively participated in the war. A leaked British Foreign and Commonwealth Office memorandum in 2004 said that that the situation in Iraq had played 'a significant role in creating a feeling of anger and impotence among especially the younger generation of British Muslims', and that this had been 'a key driver behind recruitment by extremist organisations'.[11]

However, the link between government policies and radicalisation may be counterintuitive. The European country that has been the most accommodating in relation to Muslim faith practices – Britain – is also the one with the largest extremist population. French Muslims, on the other hand, who are banned from wearing religious symbols (most prominently, of course, the headscarf) in many public spaces and often encounter open hostility when wanting to build houses of worship, seem to be far less susceptible to the ideology of the Islamist militant movement. In fact, the

Pew Global Attitudes Survey in 2006 showed that – despite the many diffi-culties they are confronted with in being practicing Muslims in a strongly secular state – the percentage of French Muslims who consider themselves French first and Muslim only second (42%) is far higher than the percent-age of British Muslims who view themselves as British first and Muslim only second (7%).[12] It is far from clear, therefore, whether 'being nice' to Muslims always produces the desired result of reducing the appeal of extremist ideologies.

The four variables assessed here are essential to understanding the different trajectories of radicalisation and recruitment among European Muslim communities. It is equally important, however, to make sense of the Islamic militant movement itself and explain how it operates in Europe.

The Islamist militant movement

Since the terrorist attacks of 11 September 2001, many attempts have been made to explain what the Islamist militant movement, often popularly but inaccurately referred to as 'al-Qaeda', represents. Historically, it emerged from the group of foreign fighters who had supported the mujahadeen in their successful campaign against the Soviet occupation of Afghanistan in the 1980s. The term 'al-Qaeda', which emerged in 1988 and translates as 'the base', initially referred to some of the so-called Afghan Arabs who had gone through certain training camps in Afghanistan and agreed to form part of an Islamic 'rapid reaction force' – ready to support local forces wherever Muslim lands were threatened by foreign invasion or occupa-tion. At the time, little was known about the group, nor is it entirely clear whether all those who had been included in al-Qaeda were conscious that they had become members of a new organisation.[13]

In fact, to this day, government analysts disagree as to which events should be regarded as the first al-Qaeda attacks. The British government, for example, begins its al-Qaeda chronology with the first World Trade Center attacks in February 1993 followed by an incident in the Philippines in 1994[14] and the four-month bombing campaign carried out by Algerian Islamists in France in 1995.[15] The US State Department's *Global Patterns of Terrorism* report, on the other hand, starts with three bombings carried out in Yemen in December 1992 and the 'Black Hawk Down' incident in Somalia in 1993 and lists no further al-Qaeda attacks until the US Embassy bombings in East Africa in August 1998.[16]

The differing accounts of the group's origins reflect a deeper disagree-ment – apparently even between the two closest allies in the 'war on terror'

– about what kind of structure al-Qaeda represents. In the period immediately following the 11 September 2001 attacks, al-Qaeda was portrayed as a hierarchical organisation with a clear chain of command and control: it resembled a spider web, with Osama bin Laden at the centre and sleeper cells around the world, prepared to strike at Western targets at any moment.[17] Quickly, this idea gave way to the notion of al-Qaeda as a 'franchise' operation. According to both the French political scientist Olivier Roy and the British terrorism analyst Peter Bergen, rather than al-Qaeda itself being involved in the planning and carrying out of terrorist attacks, the al-Qaeda leadership merely sponsored acts of terrorism, subcontracting them to local groups who were given permission to take action on behalf of the wider movement.[18] Others believed that it was wrong to understand al-Qaeda as a coherent organisation at all. They argued that it was an ideology which could be claimed by anyone who identified with certain beliefs. From this perspective, al-Qaeda represented 'an amorphous [social] movement held together by a loosely networked transnational constituency'.[19]

The three images described here – spider web, franchise and social movement – can be seen as competing visions. In reality, though, they may each represent a partially accurate understanding of al-Qaeda. In one of the best appreciations of al-Qaeda, the British journalist Jason Burke argues that the group operates at three levels: the 'hard core' (also referred to as 'al-Qaeda Central'), consisting of Bin Laden, his deputy and their lieutenants; the 'network', made up of mujahadeen who took part in active 'jihad' or spent longer periods in training camps in Afghanistan and Pakistan and have returned to their home countries; and the wider 'movement' of all those who identify with al-Qaeda's ideology and are prepared to act on al-Qaeda Central's messages and instructions while having no direct association with its members and, at best, loose connections to the 'network'.[20]

Burke emphasises that the relationship between the three levels has never been static, and that the interplay between the various layers of the organisation explains the movement's changing dynamics. Burke's observations are corroborated by the writings of Abu Musab al Suri, one of al-Qaeda's leading military thinkers, who argued that the diffusion of the movement that took place in the wake of the Western invasion of Afghanistan in late 2001 was highly desirable. According to Al Suri, al-Qaeda is meant to be 'a system, not an organisation'.[21] Consequently, the only link between the hard core and the wider movement ought to be 'a common aim, a common doctrinal program and a … self-educational program'.[22]

Experts debate which of Burke's three levels most accurately describes the structures of the Islamist militant movement in Europe. Some argue

Table 1: **Cell typology**

	Autonomy	**Selection**
Chain of command	Directed	Top-down
Guided	Takes initiative, but seeks approval	Self-recruited, but 'link to jihad'
Self-starter	Autonomous	Self-selected

that Islamist militants in Europe continue to be organised in structured cells which depend on the al-Qaeda 'hard core' in Pakistan for strategic direction and resources.[23] Others believe that the Islamist militant movement in Europe has mutated into a more autonomous phenomenon consisting of groups of alienated, 'home-grown' Muslims – sometimes also described as 'self-starters'[24] – who are using the language of al-Qaeda but largely act on their own accord.

As with the debate about al-Qaeda more generally, some of the seemingly contradictory ideas are not, in fact, mutually exclusive. On the contrary, the two positions can be integrated into a new model in which they represent 'ideal types' that are located at opposite ends of a spectrum. On this spectrum, the degree to which a terrorist cell relies on strategic direction and resources from the hard core (autonomy) and how it has been recruited (selection) determine its location between the two poles. As a result, three types of Islamist militant cell can be identified (see Table 1):

- In the 'chain of command' cell, the recruitment is 'top down' in the sense of being directed by a senior associate of the hard core who has identified suitable individuals and integrated them into the cell according to their skill, dedication, general profile and – of course – the operational requirements. The cell is fully equipped and funded by the network, which supplies money, external expertise, weapons and bomb-making materials. Importantly, some, if not all, members of the cell are sent for terrorist training abroad. The cell becomes active only if ordered to do so by the hard core.
- The 'guided cell' is largely self-recruited, often relying on what the American psychologist (and former intelligence officer) Marc Sageman correctly identified as 'cliques', that is, small-scale networks based on friends and kin.[25] Through personal contacts or active 'seeking out', 'guided cells' manage to establish some connection with the al-Qaeda network, which means that they can be integrated into the wider movement. Though it remains largely self-sufficient, such 'links to the jihad' make it possible for guided cells to benefit from some central resources, such as strategic direc-

tion, finance, and – in some cases – training abroad. Guided cells often see themselves as part of the movement, and they will be keen, therefore, to operate within the strategic parameters set out by the hard core. In practical terms, this means that they will seek guidance, or submit plans for 'approval', before they act.

- The third type of cell consists of genuine self-starters. They are self-recruited and maintain no formal or informal association with the al-Qaeda network. Similar in many respects to street gangs,[26] the cell have no access to resources from the wider movement, which means that they are entirely self-reliant in terms of funding, training and planning. Members of self-starter cells may be inspired by statements from al-Qaeda leaders such as Osama bin Laden and Ayman al-Zawahiri, and they may seek contact with other members elsewhere (hence, the Internet being described as the 'virtual glue' that holds such seemingly leaderless cells together)[27] but they define their own agenda and decide for themselves when they wish to act.

Even with this typology, however, it will sometimes be difficult to determine the nature of a particular cell, especially those that seem to fall somewhere between 'guided cell' and self-starter. Cells often appear to be genuine self-starters or amateurs until further investigations reveal more about their background, associations and links into the wider network. The nature of the cells which carried out the 2004 attacks in Madrid, for example, continues to be disputed despite years of investigation, several trials and numerous convictions in court.[28] The same is true for the London bombings in 2005 and the attacks in London and Glasgow in June 2007,[29] as well as the Dutch Hofstad group (one of whose members killed the film-maker Theo van Gogh), which some have described as a nihilistic street gang with no structure and no formalised recruitment, but which others have referred to as a highly networked, ideologically conscious group with international links.[30]

The argument about leadership and autonomy in the Islamist militant movement has recently been the subject of a fierce debate between two prominent American terrorism experts, Marc Sageman and Bruce Hoffman. Sageman argues that 2003 marked the beginning of a new phase of 'leaderless jihad' in which formal hierarchies no longer matter: 'Each local network carries out its attacks without coordination from above… [al-Qaeda] lacks a firm overarching strategy, [yet] it still has an agenda … maintaining a weak appearance of unity'.[31] By contrast, Bruce Hoffman highlights recent intelligence assessments which demonstrate that the al-Qaeda hard core has regrouped in the tribal areas of Pakistan, reasserting some of the control which it had lost in recent years. Even where Islamist terror campaigns appear to be carried out by seemingly leaderless groups, such as in Europe, such activities had resulted from the 'deliberate, long-standing subversion by Al Qaeda'.[32] Many of the attempted terrorist plots in Europe, Hoffman points out, could be traced back to Pakistan, where members of the allegedly 'leaderless' jihad had received guidance, direction and training. Al-Qaeda, he concludes, 'is a remarkably agile and flexible organization that exercises both top-down and bottom-up planning and operational capabilities'.[33]

Hoffman and Sageman agree that genuine self-starter groups – if they do exist – are less likely to pose a strategic threat to the governments or societies against which their operations are directed. Because they have no access to the resources and/or strategic leadership of a network, their operations will be less dramatic, have less impact, or fail altogether. According to Sageman, for instance, it is inconceivable for a self-starter group to carry out a highly complex operation like the 11 September 2001 attacks against the United States.[34] At the same time, most analysts concur that self-starter groups are more difficult to detect and control than 'guided' or 'chain of command' cells. While they may be less proficient at operational security, having established no links with the wider network and having no known associations with terrorist suspects, the chances that they have come to the attention of the authorities is low. Also, with no clear input from the central leadership, their operations are less easy to predict and protect against.[35]

Most contemporary analyses of the phenomenon are vague when it comes to assessing the underlying factors that have driven the evolution of the Islamist militant movement in recent years. If the drivers behind Islamist militant radicalisation and recruitment have become more diffuse, how is this manifested? What would explain the trend away from 'chain of command' cells? Has it resulted from successes in the 'war on terror' abroad, or is it that – back in Europe – efforts to conduct top-down recruitment have become more difficult? It is precisely the recent process of diffusion and change in the Islamist militant movement which the following chapters hope to explain.

CHAPTER TWO

Recruitment Grounds

Some of the most frequently asked questions about terrorist recruitment relate to specific places. The image of terrorist 'recruitment grounds' – typically mosques – where 'spotters' lurk for their victims seems to have a powerful attraction. Equally simple, then, is the perceived solution to the problem of terrorist recruitment and violent extremism more generally, which is to close down or 'clean up' all the places where such activities are thought to be carried out.

In reality, of course, the issue is somewhat more complex. There are three categories of place which may be relevant to the recruitment process. First are 'places of congregation', which are significant for no other reason than they are places where many ordinary Muslims may be found. The mosque is a typical example, and it has been significant to the recruitment process, though its role has evolved. A second category involves 'places of vulnerability', where Muslims may experience stress and alienation and are therefore potentially vulnerable to extremist approaches. One of the most important places of vulnerability – the prison – is examined in some detail. But other locations – universities, sports agencies, welfare centres – are also significant for recruitment.

'Recruitment magnets' may be found in places of both congregation and vulnerability. Their significance is that they provide 'seekers' – that is, people who have self-radicalised and are looking for opportunities to join up with the movement – with a well-known place to go. In the past, typical recruitment magnets included radical mosques and, to a lesser extent, radical bookshops.

Mosques

Many outsiders mistakenly assume that mosques are simply places of worship. In reality, though, they perform many additional functions. The mosque plays a central role in the lives of practising Muslims, as not just as a place for spiritual enrichment but also as a place where the community congregates, welfare and educational functions are performed, and generations interact. In most cases, mosques are supervised by a committee and managed by an imam, but they are open to all kinds of Muslim community and interest groups which may use the space as a venue for their own events and activities. Given the central role of the mosque in the life of Muslim communities, it should come as no surprise that extremists have been found to operate in the mosque environment, and that they have tried to exploit mosques as a place to mobilise support and recruit followers.

Until the early 2000s, the objective of many leaders of the Islamist militant movement in Europe was to take of control of certain mosques and turn them into hubs for extremist recruitment and operations. In 2002, the Dutch domestic intelligence agency claimed that extremists were hoping to establish mosques as places for fundraising and logistic support, with the additional hope of attracting recruits, the aim being to 'monitor [them] closely in the early stages and ... offer facilities'[1] to support their integration into the movement. Some of these attempts were successful, as in cases like the al-Quds mosque in Hamburg, the Islamic Cultural Centre in Milan, and the Finsbury Park mosque in London, which all became associated with the propagation of violent extremism. These mosques became recruitment magnets for radicalised individuals, who would seek out such places as a way of identifying links to the jihad. In other words, radical mosques such as these facilitated self-recruitment.[2]

In many cases, however, taking over mosques did not prove possible. The tactics used by Islamist militants to infiltrate mosques and recruit followers included presenting themselves as distinguished scholars of Islam who offered to lead prayer; setting up study groups in which they could advance their message whilst hiding their motives until close personal relationships had been formed;[3] and, of course, simply 'sit[ting] in the corner, wait[ing] for the prayer to end, and then approach individuals'[4] who had attracted their interest. None of this remained hidden from the rest of the congregation for very long. A Muslim community worker from East London recalled a typical situation as follows:

> Occasionally, they would get into an argument with you, or you
> could overhear them talking. We knew who they were. People
> who'd fallen for their message could be recognised. They were
> moving away from the mainstream. They no longer attended
> study circles. And when they did, they started asking questions
> that were provocative. They became argumentative.[5]

In some mosques, such as Brixton Mosque in south London, long-running
battles were the result. Where mosque committees took a stand and
expelled the extremists, they frequently shifted their activities from the
inside to the outside of the mosques, where they stood waiting for the end
of prayers with leaflets in their hands.[6]

In addition to attempting to take over or infiltrate mosques, a third
scenario for recruitment in mosques has involved mosques providing the
setting in which cliques were formed which then, for whatever reason,
collectively embarked on the path towards violent extremism. Perhaps this
should come as no surprise, given the role of the mosque as a centre for
discussion among practicing Muslims. As one radical explained:

> The community cannot be dissociated from the mosque ... [I]t
> is the geometrical centre of our lives ... Within our mosque, we
> don't talk about political affairs as such ... But ... the political
> and the religious are inseparable in Islam. So, whilst we don't
> talk about politics, the imam asks us in his sermons and appeals
> to take a stand against the political aggressions and the calling
> into question of Muslims in general and Islam in particular.[7]

Another radical expressed similar views:

> How can one be a good Muslim? Must one go to Iraq to defend
> one's religious brothers? Must they be avenged there? Or
> wouldn't it be better to spread the true Islam among our 'lost
> brothers' influenced by the media which broadcast a false image
> of Islam? The mosque is the cohabitation of a series of ques-
> tions.[8]

The mosque, in other words, was a natural place for some Muslims to
seek clarification and discuss seemingly confusing events such as the 11
September 2001 attacks as well as the foreign invasions that followed.

It is understandable, then, that mosques have sometimes provided the
setting for the emergence of radical groups, but this is far from saying that
they have been 'breeding grounds' for terrorists. Take, for example, the

extremist group that was based in the nineteenth arrondissement of Paris, which initially met at the Iqra mosque in the suburb of Levallois-Perret. When several French citizens who were linked to the group were killed and some detained in Iraq in early 2004,[9] the French authorities decided to take action against the mosque, assuming that it was a 'radical mosque' similar to Finsbury Park in London or al-Quds in Hamburg. In reality, though, the Iqra mosque had merely provided a meeting place for the group. Instead of shutting down the group, the closure of the mosque only prompted it to move on to another mosque, Adda'wa, which – being located in the nineteenth arrondissement – was, in fact, a more convenient place for many of the members who lived nearby.[10] Following further arrests in early 2005, it turned out that the Islamist militant network had escaped the mosque committee's attention. When interviewed by Le Monde, one of the mosque administrators stated: 'On Fridays, 3,000 people come here to pray. The rector [of the mosque] is a moderate man by nature. But he can't control everything.'[11]

In recent years, the role played by mosques in the recruitment of violent extremists has changed, with the result that much previously overt recruitment activity has been driven underground. Three developments have been instrumental in prompting this change. Firstly, most of the radical mosques, which served as recruitment magnets, no longer exist. They were variously shut down or taken over by more moderate leaders. Secondly, following the terrorist attacks in Madrid and London and various attempted attacks in other European countries, many mosque committees started paying more attention and, in some cases, clamping down on extremist activities in their mosques, resulting in 'zero tolerance' policies towards recruitment. Thirdly, many European Muslims have come to believe that most mosques are now under constant surveillance by the police and the intelligence services, which in the majority of cases is untrue, but may have had the effect of deterring extremists.

As a result, while the mosque environment continues to be used by extremists for the purpose of recruitment, extremists will move away from the mosque as soon as a first contact has been made and pursue the radicalisation of individuals in closed locations, particularly private flats and makeshift prayer halls. There is plenty of anecdotal evidence that members of Islamist militant groups continue to mix with worshippers, but – in contrast to earlier periods – they no longer attempt to start arguments or seek open confrontations, but rather try to operate quietly by befriending people individually and drawing them closer into their circle. According to a British Muslim community leader:

> They aren't picking arguments anymore. They will withdraw
> … They will not be as vocal and vociferous as they used to be,
> because they know that there is a lot of attention being paid to
> extremism, by people at the mosque but also by the authori-
> ties.[12]

This pattern of withdrawal from open agitation is consistent across
Western Europe. Mosques in Spain continue to be frequented by extremists, but potential recruits are now invited to private study group sessions
as soon as a promising relationship has been established.[13] Similarly, critics
of the extensive mosque monitoring programme in France have argued
that the authorities are failing to capture many of the 'semi-hidden places
of worship' which have recently sprung up and operate 'below the radar
of the state surveillance system'.[14] Hence, whilst some of the recruitment
magnets have been eliminated, the problem of recruitment in places of
worship may not have gone away completely.

Prisons

Prisons stand in stark contrast to mosques as recruiting environments. The
situation could hardly be more paradoxical: while prisons are confined
spaces in which access and movement is heavily restricted, mosques
are perhaps the least controllable environment imaginable. Yet there is
growing evidence that prisons – prototypical 'places of vulnerability' – have
become a uniquely conducive place for radicalisation and recruitment. As
this section will show, over time the problems associated with extremist
recruitment in prisons are likely to become more, not less, pressing.

It makes sense to repeat some of the insights that have already emerged
regarding Islam and European prisons.[15] The first – and perhaps most
obvious – point is that prisons are highly unsettling environments in
which people are confronted with existential questions. This explains why
more people convert to religion in prisons than in any other environment:
religion provides certainty, security and answers to some of the fundamental questions which inmates are likely to ask themselves. Needless to
say, embracing a new faith also signals a break with the past. Secondly,
prison conversions to Islam by non-Muslims and non-practicing Muslims[16]
far outnumber conversions to any other faith.[17] It is far from easy to say
why Islam seems to attract more converts than other faiths. Some experts
believe that it is the simplicity of its message and the ease with which one
can become Muslim that explains part of its attraction.[18] Others argue that,
especially in recent years, Islam has become a symbol of defiance of 'the

system' – an act of rebellion. According to the French sociologist Farhad Khosrokhavar: 'Islam is becoming in Europe, especially France, the religion of the repressed, what Marxism was in Europe at one time'.[19]

In some European countries, especially France and Britain, recent years have seen the emergence of radical Islamic prison gangs, which – though not always overtly political in their outlook – are highly aggressive in their rhetoric and adhere to the strict behavioural codes of the Islamist militant movement. Two elements seem to play an important role in individuals' willingness to join such groups. On the one hand, these groups provide new inmates who are completely on their own with a social network, which – in the prison environment – can be of existential importance: it enables them to avoid isolation and offers them protection against other prisoners. On the other hand, joining an Islamic group – as opposed to other 'gangs' that may operate in prison environments – gives members a unique sense of strength and superiority. Whilst publicly breaking with the past and embracing a purer *raison d'être*, they are still far from compliant with the system. On the contrary, in many cases, it seems as if their newfound identity makes them even more vociferous in their defiance of the rules and regulations to which they are subject. Indeed, as several of the officials who were interviewed in the course of the research have made clear, the groups' combination of quiet aggression with 'jihadist' rhetoric produces a sense of fear and respect among fellow prisoners as well as prison staff.[20]

It is difficult to determine precisely to what extent Muslim prison gangs should be considered full members of the Islamist militant movement. Some have no links to any specific group or network on the outside, which implies that – once released – members may become 'seekers' who will try to establish a connection with the movement on their own. Others, however, are believed to contain 'links to the jihad' which may facilitate individuals' integration into the Islamist militant structures after their release.

There are two ways in which such 'links to the jihad' inside prison can be established and maintained. One is through so-called 'radical imams' who claim to provide religious instruction for inmates.[21] Most European governments have recognised the problem, but – though it may be relatively easy to expel imams who are suspected of promoting extremism from prison – it has proved difficult to provide adequate alternative providers of Islamic religious instruction. Many governments have decided to adopt certification schemes, whereby only 'vetted' imams are permitted access to prisons. At the same time, with Islam being a congregational faith that requires no formal qualifications for spiritual leadership, there is a risk that legitimate providers of religious instruction will be marginalised. In the words of a Spanish police adviser, 'Many of these people are completely unknown, and we don't have the resources or ability to find out who they are'.[22]

Furthermore, certification schemes can take many years to implement, which – in practice – could mean that large parts of the Muslim prison population are being cut off from religious instruction altogether. Nowhere is the problem more obvious than in France. A national Muslim prison chaplain has been appointed and a certification scheme is now in place. Even so, with more than 50% of the French prison population estimated to be Muslim and fewer than 100 imams officially 'certified' in early 2007, it will take several years until the demand is met.[23] Where no religious instruction can be provided, inmates are often left to their own devices. Ordinary prison staff are not always sufficiently trained to spot instances of radicalisation and recruitment, and will – in any case – be unable to do so when it is undertaken in a foreign language.[24]

A second way in which 'links to the jihad' can be established is through Islamist militant inmates themselves. They are in a good position to facilitate connections to networks on the outside, but – more importantly – their reputation will help them to attract recruits inside prison. A Dutch prison guard, referring to one of the members of the Hofstad group for whom he had responsibility, commented that other prisoners were '[adoring him] like a prophet, they literally kiss his feet'.[25] Some of the officials interviewed confirmed this impression, saying that Islamist militants entered prison 'with a certain amount of notoriety. They come in there as heroes.'[26]

In the immediate future, the problem of radicalisation and recruitment within prisons is likely to worsen. With the exception of France, no Western European country had a significant Islamist militant prisoner population before 2001. In the following years – and ironically, as a result of the success in fighting terrorism and pursuing offenders through the courts – the extremist prisoner population has increased substantially. In countries like Britain and Spain, for example, there are now several hundred individuals in prison who are either awaiting trial or have been convicted of terrorist offences.[27] While many resources are being used to monitor and control the most high-profile of these individuals, little is done about those who are convicted of lesser offences. Yet it is members of the latter group which should be the greatest cause of concern: not only are they likely to engage in radicalisation and recruitment whilst in prison, they are also the ones who will be released within relatively short periods of time, sometimes after only two or three years.

Table 2: **Typology of 'recruitment grounds'**

	Places of congregation	**Places of vulnerability**	**Recruitment 'magnets'**
Significance/ function	No particular significance other than Muslims meeting	Taking advantage of individuals' crises or lack of orientation	Attracting 'seekers' from a wider area
Examples	• Mosques • Internet cafes • Cafeterias • Gyms • Summer camps	• Prisons • Refugee centres • Welfare agencies • Universities	• 'Radical mosques' • 'Radical bookshops'

Some European countries – for example, Spain – have entertained the idea of concentrating the Islamist militant prisoner population in specific prisons, thus ensuring better control and preventing contact with ordinary delinquents, but – in the longer term – this approach (known as 'concentrate and isolate') may turn out to be counter-productive by providing Islamist militants with a focus for their efforts to portray Islamist militants as 'political prisoners' and European governments as 'anti-Muslim'. Though the problem has been recognised, no European government has yet managed to put together a coherent strategy for countering radicalisation and recruitment in prisons.[28]

Other locations

Many other places have played a role in Islamist militant recruitment. In principle, of course, recruitment can take place anywhere, but the vast majority of places which have been mentioned in relation to recruitment in Europe fall into one of the two broad categories identified earlier: they are either places of congregation, or places of vulnerability (see Table 2).

Hence, places of vulnerability in which Muslims are likely to lack orientation or experience tensions and personal crises include not just prisons but also places such as asylum-seeker reception centres and residences, which the Dutch intelligence services in 2002 highlighted as recruitment grounds;[29] and Muslim welfare organisations, which are believed to have been instrumental in forging the relationships that led to the formation of the cell that was responsible for the attacks in London and Glasgow.[30]

Many educational institutions, especially universities, can also be places of vulnerability.[31] Universities have always been centres of radical thought, of which – arguably – radical Islam represents but one incarnation. However, universities – like prisons and refugee centres – are also places where people are prone to experience feelings of isolation, loneliness and vulnerability. After all, for many young people, going to university constitutes the first significant 'break' in their lives, which involves leaving their parents' house, moving to a different city, and building a new circle of friends and social relations. As Baber Siddiqi of the British-based Luqmann Institute put it: 'When young Muslims go to university, they often feel a sense of insecurity and so the radical groups provide a social forum and then develop personal relationships'.[32]

In addition, of course, there are plenty of places of congregation, such as Internet cafes, cafeterias and fitness centres in the Muslim areas of big European cities, as well as summer camps organised by Muslim youth organisations. None of these environments are inherently significant or dangerous in and by themselves, but they can be turned into 'recruitment grounds' for the purpose of turning people towards violent extremism.

Certain Islamic bookshops, which in the past have played a role similar to that of radical mosques as recruitment magnets attracting seekers from a wider geographical area, are exceptions to the pattern. Like radical mosques, some Islamic bookshops managed to establish a reputation for making available 'jihadist' literature and videos as well as recordings from radical preachers. Most of these materials can nowadays be found on the Internet, but one must not forget that such places have been significant not just as distributors of propaganda materials but – more importantly – as meeting points which have allowed like-minded individuals to connect socially and identify 'links to the jihad'.

It would be a mistake to look for particular places as typical 'recruitment grounds'. While governments are well advised to prevent the emergence of recruitment magnets such as radical mosques and bookshops, in general it is more useful to think of geographical places in terms of their social functions, that is, as places of vulnerability or places of congregation. Wherever Muslims meet or experience feelings of isolation and vulnerability, recruitment is possible. What matters at least as much as the precise geographical location are the people involved in the process. So, who are the recruiters, and how do they operate?

CHAPTER THREE

The Recruiters

In media and fictional accounts, it is the recruiter who is portrayed as leading the process of recruitment. He spots and selects potential candidates, who are then ideologically seduced and brainwashed into joining the movement. In reality, though, the process of joining a violent extremist movement is a complex social activity in which both sides – the recruiter and the recruit – play active roles. Drawing on research conducted by the Italian sociologist Donatella della Porta as well as his own findings, Sageman shows that popular characterisations of recruitment are highly misleading, noting that recruiters more often play the role of gatekeepers than 'lurking in mosques, ready to subvert naive and passive worshippers'.[1]

While certain myths about recruiters have already been dispelled,[2] it would be wrong, however, to conclude that recruiters do not exist, or that they have no role to play. In Europe, certain individuals, agencies and entities appear to be more relevant in facilitating the process of recruitment than others. The focus here is on 'gateway organisations', 'radical imams', and activists. Of these, it is the activists who are the drivers of recruitment, even though gateway organisations and radical imams continue to help shape the environment that makes extremist recruitment possible.

Gateway organisations
The term 'gateway organisation' is frequently used by policymakers and intelligence officials to describe the kinds of organisations which – though

not directly involved in violence – may nevertheless facilitate individuals' movement towards violent extremism.[3] The case against them can be summed up as follows:

- Gateway organisations are not engaged in the pursuit of violence, nor do they necessarily call for violence, but they promote an ideological framework – a mindset – that justifies and legitimates the use of violence for political and religious purposes (indoctrination).
- Even if they refrain from political agitation, gateway organisations promote values and faith practices that are incompatible with democracy and the ideal of an integrated, socially cohesive society. In that sense, they sustain the conditions of exclusion and separation in which violent extremism is likely to emerge (subversion).
- Gateway organisations make it possible for individuals to socialise with radicals and become part of a milieu in which they will be exposed to violent extremists and where it will be easy to establish links to the jihad (socialisation).

Needless to say, there is a great variety of groups to which the label 'gateway organisation' has been applied, and it is often difficult to judge whether a particular group engages in subversion, indoctrination, or extremist socialisation.

Take, for example, the Jama'at al-Tabligh (Tabligh), which was founded in India in 1926 and has since become a global missionary movement whose principal aim is to propagate and revive the faith, especially among non-practicing Muslims, who are believed to have abandoned the 'right path'. Its faith practices are highly rigid and include the requirement for followers to separate 'their daily life from the "impious society" that surround[s] them'.[4] In France, the group managed to generate a broad following in the 1970s and 1980s, mainly – it seems – because of its success in 'reforming' criminals and drug addicts.[5] Though undoubtedly fundamentalist in its religious approach,[6] the Tabligh has no explicit political stance. When Omar Nasiri, a Belgian-Moroccan radical who looked for an opportunity to join al-Qaeda, turned to the group in the 1990s, he was told in no uncertain terms that 'the only true jihad is the non-violent jihad of the Tabligh'.[7]

The Tabligh have come under intense public scrutiny, because various individuals who have been arrested in connection with terrorist activities turned out to have prior associations with the group. This was true of three members of the network responsible for the Madrid train bombings in 2004,[8] and also of some of those suspected of involvement in the plot to bring down several transatlantic flights in August 2006.[9] There is no suggestion that any of these individuals were indoctrinated politically during their time with the Tabligh. Rather, the argument is that the Tabligh engage in religious practices that are near-identical to those of the Islamist militant movement, and that Islamist militants are thus presented with a religiously primed, yet otherwise empty vessel into which to insert their extremist political agenda. The Tabligh, then, can be said to be subversive and provide a degree of religious indoctrination, but there is little evidence that the group socialises members into extremist milieus.

The second example is Hizb-ut Tahrir (HT), which claims to be a political party whose principal aim is to create a global caliphate.[10] In contrast to the Tabligh, HT is overtly political. Its ideology is strikingly similar to al-Qaeda's, with differences not over aims and assumptions but mainly over strategy. For HT, the most promising means of achieving the global caliphate is not through terrorism but by infiltrating the political, administrative and military elites in key Muslim majority countries, who – as soon as a critical mass has been reached – are expected to overthrow their governments and establish Islamic regimes.[11]

Some experts have characterised HT as being composed of 'noisy but essentially harmless young people'.[12] Yet the group fulfils all three of the criteria that were mentioned earlier: it indoctrinates, it subverts and – most significantly – it introduces members to the kinds of social networks that make it easy to move from non-violent political agitation to violent extremism. According to the journalist Shiv Malik, 'These people hang out with each other, they meet each other. They have arguments, no doubt, sometimes very strong and vicious arguments, but they regard each other as brothers.'[13] In fact, not only are HT and Islamist militants part of the same 'scene', but they try to recruit each other's members. Islamist militants will join HT meetings, hoping to find members who are exhausted with the group's repetitive and seemingly never-ending political discourse. Knowing that – ideologically – there is little disagreement in principle, all they need to do is to exploit their desire for action, asking them: 'Aren't you tired of the talking?'[14]

A third example is the group al-Muhajiroun, which split from HT in 1996 and was led by the radical preacher Omar Bakri Mohammed. It has since gone through various mutations, including several name changes (usually in response to being banned), but some of its key personnel have remained the same.[15] Ideologically, the group adopted a more aggressive stance than HT, most prominently by sanctioning attacks on Western soldiers in Afghanistan and glorifying the 11 September 2001 attacks against the United States.[16] Originally based in the UK, Bakri was keen to expand the movement and opened offices in Denmark and Pakistan,[17] though much of the group's following continued to be British.

In its public statements, the group rejected any active involvement in violence. In reality, though, Bakri and his colleagues helped members to make their way to the frontlines of the 'global jihad'. Indeed, the main purpose of the group's office in Pakistan seems to have been to allow members to join the ranks of the insurgents in Afghanistan after the country had been invaded by Coalition forces in late 2001. Bakri frequently bragged that he could provide people with references that would allow them to train in terrorist camps across Asia and the Middle East.[18] Given such activities, the question is no longer whether al-Muhajiroun should be regarded as a gateway organisation, but rather whether it ought to be considered a terrorist group.

Are gateway organisations part of the problem or part of the solution? Some European governments, such as the British, have in the past been eager to cooperate with gateway organisations, arguing that they possess credibility with radicalised Muslims who would not listen to secular or even moderately religious voices, whilst others – especially the French – believe that they must never be empowered.[19]

In deciding whether gateway organisations can be friends or should always be foes, two points are worth considering. Firstly, as this section has shown, not all organisations are the same, and it will be essential for governments to evaluate each group on its own merits. Secondly, it is important to be clear about what kind of partnership is being envisaged. Working with the Tabligh, non-political Salafist groups or the 'soft' Islamists of the Muslim Brotherhood at the grassroots level could be worth exploring, but governments would be ill-advised to treat them as representatives of the Muslim community or to give them opportunities to present themselves as such. It is difficult to see how groups such as HT and al-Muhajiroun, could ever play a positive role in combating violent extremism.

Radical imams

When European newspapers report on 'radical Islam', it is often so-called 'radical imams' with their threatening demeanour and inflammatory speeches to which they refer. Moderate Muslims are understandably upset when figures such as Abu Hamza in London or Mohamed el Maghrebi in Paris are invited on television shows or interviewed in newspapers, thereby providing an image of the Muslim community which is completely distorted and likely to further anti-Muslim sentiments among the general population. At the same time, it is hard to deny that – however ridiculous some of their public appearances – radical imams have played an important role in the radicalisation and recruitment of the relatively small number of European Muslims who have joined the Islamist militant movement.

What, then, is the function of radical imams in the process of recruitment? A recent study of leadership in the European Islamist militant movement made it clear that 'radical preachers' appear as 'central nodal points' in the early stages of the formation of a terrorist network – that is, when individuals are being radicalised, recruited and connected with each other – but 'do not … feature as prominently or as decisively [at the] training or tactical planning stage'.[20] Based on this analysis, as well as the research that has been carried out for this paper, radical imams can be said to perform four main roles:

- They are the *chief propagandists* of the Islamist militant movement, who spread its messages and narratives and make them relevant to the lives of European Muslims, especially the second- and third-generation descendants of Muslim immigrants.
- They act as *religious authorities* – even when they lack any religious training or other theological credentials – by providing supposed legal rulings (fatwas) and justifications for violent jihad.
- They serve as *recruitment magnets*, whose role is to attract followers from a wider geographical area and allow them to integrate with the movement.
- They create *networks of networks*, connecting individual cells, smaller groups and networks both nationally and internationally, thus providing the 'human glue' that keeps the Islamist militant movement together.

An excellent illustration of the phenomenon of the radical imam and its different functions is Abdul Jabbar van de Ven, a 30-year-old Dutchman who converted to Islam at the age of 14. Taking advantage of a scholarship, he went to Saudi Arabia for a year, where he studied Arabic and received some rudimentary religious training. Upon his return to Holland, he started providing religious instruction for Dutch teenagers, mostly of Moroccan descent. The intention was to spread the word (*dawa*), and he quickly built up a considerable following.[21] Most of these activities were entirely legitimate, and there was no reason – at least initially – for the authorities to be concerned. Following the 11 September 2001 attacks, however, Jabbar made a name for himself when he appeared on public television, declaring his solidarity with bin Laden. When the Dutch film-maker Theo van Gogh was killed by a member of the Hofstad group, he congratulated the killer and used the opportunity to encourage Muslims to assassinate a controversial member of the Dutch parliament.

Having achieved national notoriety, Jabbar was invited to mosques and study groups across the country, which enabled him to extend his network of contacts and, increasingly, act as a matchmaker for different radical cells. Although he had no permanent link with any particular institution, his association with the radical al-Furqaan mosque in Eindhoven provided him with access to a number of international contacts, most prominently Islamist militants from North Africa.[22] Most astonishingly, although he had barely completed a year of religious studies in Saudi Arabia, Jabbar's religious rulings proved highly influential among his impressionable audience. As it turned out, one of the members of the Hofstad group, Jason Walters, claimed that Jabbar had responded to his request for a fatwa in which he declared the decapitation of the Dutch prime minister to be halal (permitted).[23] Jabbar, therefore, had not just propagated the messages and narratives of the Islamist militant movement and forged networks among extremists in Denmark; he seems to have actively incited acts of terrorist violence.

In the late 1990s and early 2000s, radical imams such as Jabbar became a familiar sight in Britain, Germany, Benelux and the Scandinavian countries, but their influence was – and continues to be – negligible in many southern European countries, such as Spain.[24] Why is this? The answer lies in the nature of the Muslim audience to which they were appealing. Radical imams were experts at articulating their followers' cultural anxieties and exploiting their conflicted sense of identity, and they did so in the (European) languages in which their second- and third-generation European Muslim audiences felt most comfortable.[25] In Spain or Italy, the vast majority of Muslims only arrived in Europe after 1990, which means that there is no anxiety-ridden second- or third-generation to appeal to (see Chapter 1). Also, being mostly North African, Muslims in southern Europe are fully fluent in Arabic, which means that they are unlikely to be impressed with the scriptural knowledge of self-taught clerics like Jabbar or Abu Hamza. This is not to say that radical imams are completely without followings in southern Europe, but rather that their appeal is bound to be limited.

Is the era of the radical imam coming to a close? There can be no doubt that, in recent years, opportunities for radical imams to spread their message and act as recruitment magnets have been reduced substantially.

Some have been deported or detained; more stringent laws have been passed against the incitement to violence, or – as in Britain – the 'glorification' of terrorism; there are fewer radical bookshops that sell their tapes; radical mosques have been closed down, and other places of worship have refused radical imams entry.

France in particular has implemented an aggressive policy aimed at curbing radical imams' activities. Whereas, for example, in Britain only clear and repeated incitement to violence would prompt the authorities to take action,[26] the French approach is to clamp down on any utterances that could be considered an 'ideological point of reference' for Islamist militants. As a consequence, dozens of imams have been deported to North Africa since 2001.[27] Critics claim that the French government's approach has been excessive, targeting not just clerics whose statements justify the actions of the Islamist militant movement but even those Salafi Muslims who have spoken out against violent extremism and believe that 'loyalty to the Prince' is one of their fundamental duties as Muslims. As one French community leader explains: 'The armed Salafist group [in Algeria] has nothing to do with [our] movement. [We are] completely different.'[28]

Even in France, though, some genuinely radical imams are still active.[29] Some of those who have left Europe continue to propagate their ideas via the Internet, using interactive chat communities, video links and services such as PalTalk through which they engage with followers and provide fatwas. The space for human interaction may have been reduced significantly, but it is clearly too early to conclude that the radical imams have gone away altogether.

Activists
A third type of actor that analysts frequently refer to when describing the process of recruitment is the 'activist'. According to the Norwegian analyst Petter Nesser, it is the 'activist' leader of a terrorist cell who 'makes things happen':

> He is typically senior to the other operatives, and central to the recruitment, radicalization and training of the other cell members. The entrepreneur has an 'activist mindset', being driven by ideas rather than personal grievances. He is interested in and committed to social issues and politics. He demands respect from his surroundings and he has a strong sense of justice … He has an 'entrepreneurial spirit' and wants to build something for himself and those he considers 'his people' …

In the end he takes on a 'project' for the holy warriors. He has high aspirations, and sometimes he has a record of failed ambitions.[30]

Nesser stresses that activists are intelligent and self-motivated, and that they use their charisma and rhetoric skills to persuade others to join the cause. The people they recruit, on the other hand, are often less capable and motivated, and may have a record of criminality.[31] Nesser's sociology of Islamist militant cell members differentiates between the leaders (the 'activist' and his younger 'protégé') and the followers (the 'drifters' and 'misfits') whom they have recruited.[32]

Nesser's analysis, together with other reports as well as the research that was conducted for this study, makes it possible to identify three main roles played by the activist:

- The activist provides leadership and cohesion. In many cases, the cell has been established by the activist, and it is he who is seen as responsible for making sure it stays together. In doing so, the activist is helped by charisma and commitment. However, normally he is not in any position to deploy religious authority.
- The activist leads the process of cell expansion and/or recruitment. Using his considerable rhetorical and social skills, he reaches out to others and persuades them to join the cause. He is also most likely to have a social network on which to draw for contacts.
- The activist is responsible for the cell's external relations.[33] He is the one who establishes contact with a 'link to the jihad', making it possible for a cell to be integrated into the wider Islamist militant movement. If successful, this process may transform a group of self-starters into a 'guided cell' with access to the resources and strategic direction of al-Qaeda.

This description applies to many leaders of Islamist militant cells which have come to the attention of the authorities, including Mohammed Siddique Khan, the leader of the cell responsible for the 7 July 2005 attacks in London; Sarhane Faket, one of the activists involved in the Madrid network; and Mohammed Bouyeri, who played a leading role in the Hofstad group.[34]

A good, but less well-known, example of activist leadership in recruitment is the case of Karin Abdelselam Mohamed and a self-starter group from Ceuta (a Spanish enclave on the coast of Morocco), which was disrupted by the Spanish police in December 2006. Karin had become radicalised in prison whilst he was serving a sentence for involvement in petty crime. After his release, he befriended a group of youths in a deprived and largely Muslim area of Ceuta. The group – which eventually had 11 members – regularly met on the grounds of a local mosque. During these meetings, the group discussed religious and political issues and watched videos from 'jihadist' battlefronts across the world.[35]

At some point, the group started to move from discussion to action, beginning by spreading rumours about an impending attack and spraying jihadist graffiti. The first – and only – act of low-level violence carried out by the group was the destruction of a tomb, which drew widespread condemnation from the local community and prompted the police to get involved. As further investigations revealed, prior to being arrested the group had contemplated spectacular attacks against a fairground, a fuel depot and a shopping mall. For this purpose, Karin had attempted to contact an individual he knew from his time in prison, who had been convicted for his role in recruiting Muslims to fight in Iraq.[36] It is, of course, impossible to say whether the cell would ever have carried out the attacks that were discussed during the meetings at the mosque, but it seems fair to say that, had Karin, the activist, succeeded in connecting with a 'link to the jihad', a group of hapless self-starters could have been transformed into a 'guided cell' with considerable potential to carry out a number of devastating attacks.

Of all the different actors and entities described in this chapter, activists such as Karin come closest to fitting the popular idea of the recruiter. But how exactly do they bind people to the group? Sageman – drawing on Della Porta's earlier research – points out that many of the cells that had been recruited by activists consisted of 'bunches of guys' who had developed intense social bonds.[37] This is also reflected in an empirical study of 242 Islamist militants in Europe that was carried out by the Dutch political scientist Edwin Bakker. He found that friendship and kinship were highly significant in driving the process of group formation.[38] And indeed, rather than religious doctrine or talk about high politics, it is more often by satisfying the deeply held material and immaterial longings of individuals that activists manage to generate group cohesion.[39] They may help to address potential recruits' practical needs,[40] for example, or they simply make them feel accepted. In the words of a French community leader:

> He [the recruit, suddenly] has a group of people that listen to him. So it makes him feel very important and very opinionated

at the same time, and therefore he has some kind of influence amongst a group of people.[41]

A number of authors have stressed the similarities between recruitment into violent extremism and into religious cults.[42] As with cults, the Islamist militant group serves a socialising function that can be strikingly similar to that of the family, with the activist playing the role of a charismatic 'father'. The British journalist Shiv Malik, who spent several months investigating the background of the 'London bombers', believes that

> people underestimate – or rather, people haven't come to appreciate – what it means to find a family again. Many of the *jihadists* broke with their parents, and they were cut off from everything. They don't want to leave the group because they don't want to be pariahs again. So the fatherly element is very important ... They hang out with each other, and they all become brothers.[43]

In this context, then, the purpose of activist-organised training camps, white-water rafting trips and paint-balling exercises (which arise repeatedly in the descriptions of how Islamist militant groups have formed) is not primarily to convey skills that may be important in 'fighting the jihad' but rather to strengthen interpersonal bonds and group identity.

In contrast to the indisputable significance of social bonds, little evidence was found for Sageman's contention that it takes an encounter with a 'link to the jihad' in order for cells to radicalise. On the contrary, in most of instances examined, radicalisation of the cell had preceded any encounters with 'links to the jihad'. Furthermore, activists were often found to take the initiative in recruiting new members for the cell, for example, by identifying and befriending potential recruits at the local mosque or by attending the meetings of gateway organisations. Sageman may be correct in highlighting the fact that recruitment for the Islamist militant is far less strategic and professional than commonly imagined, and he deserves credit for putting to rest the myth that al-Qaeda engages in systematic, top-down 'recruitment drives'. At the same time, low-level recruitment is a common occurrence, and many community leaders interviewed could cite instances in which 'spotting' by activists was unfolding before their eyes.[44]

In conclusion, it seems obvious that activists have, in recent years, driven recruitment for the Islamist militant movement in Europe. Given the slow decline of other actors – especially the radical imams – their significance is likely to increase. It is primarily activists, therefore, against whom

Table 3: **Functions of recruitment agents**

Gateway organisations	Radical imams	Activists
• Indoctrination	• Propaganda	• Leadership and group cohesion
• Socialisation	• Religious justification	• Cell expansion
• Subversion	• 'Recruitment magnets'	• 'External relations'
	• Networking	

governments' counter-recruitment efforts should be directed. In doing so, however, it will be essential not only to understand who they are but also what kind of messages they aim to use to generate support.

CHAPTER FOUR

The Message

Hundreds of articles and books have been written about the ideology of the Islamist militant movement: the subject is well explored.[1] What is of interest here is how and why this ideology resonates with those who have been recruited into the movement – in other words, the process through which the ideology is disseminated. It is the interplay between social conditions and ideology which is of particular interest.

There are three stages during which messages play a role in furthering the process of recruitment to the Islamist militant movement. The first is in creating or exploiting a personal crisis. The second is referred to as 'frame alignment' and describes the period during which individuals internalise the movement's religious and, by extension, political doctrines. The justification of violence is the third and final stage, and represents the culmination of the process.

Cognitive openings

It is well established that an individual's decision to join a violent extremist group tends to be preceded by a so-called 'tipping point' which triggers a re-evaluation of that individual's status in society, attitudes towards political and religious questions, and even sense of self. Andrew Silke, a British psychologist, argues that 'catalyst events' are essential in explaining the transition from being a largely passive member of a disaffected group to becoming a violent extremist.[2] Similarly, an American researcher, Harvey Kushner, discovered that potential suicide bombers nearly always had a relative or close friend killed or abused by the enemy, and that it was this event which caused them to conclude that retaliatory action had to be taken.[3]

More generally, Quintan Wiktorowicz, an American sociologist, claims that personal crises can produce so-called 'cognitive openings' which 'shake certainty in previously accepted beliefs and render an individual more receptive to the possibility of alternative views and perspective'.[4] Crises, he stresses, need not be political, but can equally be cultural, economic or indeed purely personal.[5]

In the research conducted for this paper, many instances could be found in which militants skilfully exploited 'tipping points' or crises in order to produce cognitive openings. There were two kinds of situation, which were encountered again and again. The first involves experiences of exclusion and discrimination in Western European society. European Muslims, especially the second and third generation, often feel that there is a wide gap between governments' inclusive rhetoric and their constant talk about equal rights on one hand, and the lack of respect and equal treatment afforded to Muslims by the societies of which they are citizens on the other hand. As one French radical explained:

> I am a French Muslim … [Yet still] I am regarded with suspicion … On a day to day level, this is what it often comes down to … The fact that, in their eyes, you are a foreigner.[6]

This kind of perception – of being regarded as a foreigner – sometimes appears to breed a form of reverse loathing. In the words of another French radical:

> The type of person who despises you is inferior to me … be it moral, academic and even material. He's a dead loss, less than nothing. If this person who despises me [was] better than me, I would understand. Then, I would say there was good reason. But, in reality, some of these people have feelings of unmotivated hatred that seem to be part of their very essence.
>
> *Do you have to deal with this kind of annoyance at work?*
>
> I deal with it in the street, on public transport, when dealing with local government, everywhere.[7]

Violent extremists have long understood that such experiences can be exploited in order to attract people into the Islamist militant movement. As Omar Bakri, the leader of al-Muhajiroun, put it:

> If there [was] no racism in the West, there [would be] no conflict
> of identity. People, when they suffer in the West, it makes them
> think. If there [was] no discrimination or racism, I think it would
> be very difficult for us.[8]

In this kind of situation, Islamist militants can offer 'identities of empower-
ment' which allow individuals to reconstruct their sense of self and gain
new confidence. When interviewed by Wiktorowicz, Bakri said that he
would respond to recruits' experiences of exclusion by saying: 'Come on
Abu Jafar. You are not Bobby. You belong to a very great nation [Islam].
You belong to the history of civilisation, 1,300 years of a ruling [Islamic]
system.'[9]

Young Muslims' sense of alienation from Western society is often
mirrored in an equally strong conflict with their parents' culture – the
second type of situation that can lead to a cognitive opening. During the
first wave of Muslim settlement in Western Europe – in the 1950s and 1960s
– Muslims imported and maintained many customs such as arranged
marriages which they believed to be Islamic, though – in reality – they
were mostly local traditions and had little to do with scholarly understand-
ings of Islam. As time went by, it became obvious that these traditions
made little sense in the context of late modern Western societies, and
the second and third generation started to challenge them. This is what
happened in the case of the London bombers. According to British journalist Shiv Malik, who spent several months in the hometown of Mohammed
Siddique Khan:

> [Khan] felt that … women should have access to university
> education, and that forced marriages were wrong. He also made
> a stance against corruption and the anti-meritocratic attitude
> within his community … Later on, people would say that he
> had been thrown out of the mosque because he was a radical,
> but really it was because he was challenging the [social] status
> quo.[10]

As with many others, Khan's response to the conflict with his parents and
his community, who all insisted that their 'way of life' was the correct – that
is, Islamic – way, was to educate himself. In the process, he encountered
and embraced the purist and seemingly far more rational interpretations
of Islam that were offered by the Wahhabi and Salafi traditions. Equipped
with his newfound knowledge, he was then able to expose traditional
institutions such as forced marriage as un-Islamic.

Against this background, it becomes easy to understand why the idea of a global community of believers – the *umma* – has such appeal for second- and third-generation European Muslims, who feel squeezed between Western society and the culture of their parents: it confidently articulates a counterpoint to Western society, yet it simultaneously challenges the narrowness of the 'cultural Islam' imported into Europe by the first generation of Muslim immigrants in the 1950s and 1960s. In Malik's view, much of the literature produced by organisations like Hizb-ut Tahrir and other extremist groups is aimed precisely at capitalising on this conflict of identity.[11]

In many cases, of course, extremist groups are hoping to induce crises or 'tipping points' rather than wait for them to materialise. This, one may argue, is the primary purpose of the 'jihadist' videos from battlefronts such as the North Caucasus, Palestine, Afghanistan and Iraq, which can be downloaded from the Internet but also continue to be shown at events in community centres, mosques, universities and private homes. These films perform a number of important functions. They provoke 'moral outrage'[12] among their audience and produce a sense of what Khosrokhavar describes as 'humiliation by proxy'.[13] But they also introduce viewers to the grand narrative of the 'war against Islam', which – according to these videos – is a war against every Muslim. In doing so, they convey the need for urgent action – the imperative, in other words, to stand up for other Muslims, who appear to face suffering and systematic injustices if not extermination and genocide.

According to several officials from Britain and France who were interviewed, jihadist videos have recently begun to weave together scenes from international jihad battlefronts with Western experiences that appeal directly to a second- and third-generation European Muslim audience.[14] As a result, such videos become powerful 'sense-makers', suggesting that European Muslims' experiences of alienation, crisis and exclusion can be blamed on the same powerful forces responsible for the suffering of Muslims elsewhere, so that – in the viewers' perception – a young Muslim in a Parisian suburb and an Iraqi insurgent all become part of one and the same struggle.

Frame alignment

Having exploited a cognitive opening, recruits are made to undergo a learning period which is often referred to as 'frame alignment' by social movement theorists. The aim of frame alignment is to achieve convergence between the views of the recruits and the movement's grand narrative.[15]

In the case of the Islamist militant movement, the religious nature of the movement's core ideas and principles has important implications for how the group and its individual members function, as well as for the kinds of actions they are likely to engage in.

Firstly, being religious in nature, any of the new ideas and principles that are communicated during the process of frame alignment are supposedly absolute and all-embracing. They require the recruits' total submission. Indeed, some of the radicals interviewed emphasised not only that Islam recognises no distinction between religion and the state, but also that there is no boundary between the public and the private.[16] From the extremists' point of view, therefore, being a 'good Muslim' calls for an absolute commitment and allows for no questioning or doubts once the religious validity of an idea or a practice has been established.

Secondly, the religious component of Islamist militancy postulates that members live in an impure society and that, consequently, all ties with their friends and family – unless, of course, they are part of the movement – need to be cut off. Recruits, in other words, need to isolate themselves from the society that surrounds them, because practically everyone who does not adhere to the group's rigid religious rules or share their political views is regarded as *kuffar* (infidel) or *takfir* (apostate). Indeed, close interaction with society is regarded as dangerous, so that – if anything – the process of frame alignment will intensify the in-group dynamics.

Thirdly, what makes Islamist militants different from other 'fundamentalist' groups such as the Tabligh is their emphasis on armed struggle – that is, violent jihad – to liberate and unite Muslim lands under Islamic rule. The urgent need for 'jihad' runs like a thread through the process of frame alignment. Regardless of its many, more peaceful meanings,[17] Islamist militants present 'jihad' in almost exclusively military terms. The concept is portrayed as one of the principal religious duties which every able-bodied Muslim male should pursue. When confronted with objections and doubts, Islamist militants will emphasise that as long as innocent Muslims are being killed and the *umma* is under attack, most forms of violent 'jihad' qualify as 'defensive' and are therefore legitimate in religious terms.

Many of the videos and tapes that are shown during the frame alignment period are designed to sustain the argument about the supposedly 'true meaning' of jihad. For example, when the police sifted through the belongings of the members of the Madrid network, numerous tapes of radical preachers were found. What they all had in common was their emphasis on the virtues of 'jihad', and their criticism of those who failed to respond to the call. The Jordanian-born cleric Abu Qatada, who currently lives in London, was among the most strident advocates of this position. In his tapes, he consistently argued that 'jihad' was not simply a religious duty in response to the Western attack against the *umma*, but an action that would generate great rewards for those who engaged in it. In his own words: 'Those who fall in the name of God and their nation do not die, because they remain alive with God'.[18]

Social movement theory claims that success in achieving frame alignment depends on the credibility of the 'frame articulator' as much as it requires particular messages to be persuasive.[19] This helps in understanding why many radical imams' lack of scholarly qualifications matters less than might be expected. Members of the Islamist militant movement are highly distrustful of 'official scholarship', which they believe has been corrupted by the Middle East's autocratic regimes.[20] For self-taught or renegade clerics, then, having battlefront experience can be as important as a means of gaining credibility as any theological certificate. Furthermore, converts, second- and third-generation European Muslims, and North Africans whose Arabic has lapsed frequently equate the most rudimentary knowledge of the Arabic language with great scholarship. As a British community leader told us:

> [The radical imams] could speak English, they knew the lingo, the slang … But they could also delve into the Quran and read the Arabic. Reading the Quran in Arabic is like music to Muslims' ears, especially to British converts who are unable to understand the context and who are likely to be impressed by people who pretend to be Islamic scholars and who speak Arabic.[21]

Indeed, Abdul Jabbar van de Veen, who had spent barely a year studying Arabic and receiving religious instruction in Saudi Arabia, made no secret of his lack of theological knowledge. He told a Dutch newspaper: 'In the land of the blind, the one-eyed is king'.[22]

Justifying violence

The learning process of recruits culminates in accepting the justifications for violence. One of the critical preconditions is recruits' full identification with the *umma* rather than the (European) societies in which they are living. According to one of the radicals interviewed, the *umma* 'transcends the individual … [it] exists all over the world and its troubles are felt the same way everywhere'.[23] As a result, recruits believe they have a stake in all conflicts between Muslims and non-Muslims regardless of where they take place. In the words of the same radical:

> Every Muslim is angry when the *umma* is being undermined. I
> am going to give you the example of the demonstrations against
> the Vatican in Arab countries [in 2006].... Western politicians
> became upset about this ... [But,] how can you ask me not to
> get angry when the *umma* is being tarnished? How can they be
> proud of their nations and not understand that we are proud of
> ours?[24]

In fact, understanding recruits' strong and exclusive identification with
the *umma* explains how 'home-grown' terrorists can bring themselves
to launch attacks against their own communities. Despite their close
geographical proximity, they no longer feel they are part of these communities: they see themselves as citizens of the *umma*, surrounded by infidel
'others' whose principal aim and motivation is to suppress members of
their nation.

The next step, then, is to respond to the troubles of the *umma*, and
recruits will have learned that the religiously correct response to assaults
against the *umma* is 'jihad'. Whenever Muslims or Muslim lands are
attacked or occupied, Islamist militant doctrine dictates that the means
taken to respond to such an attack qualify as 'defensive jihad' in which
every Muslim has an individual duty to participate. This doctrine applies
even when traditional scholars speak out against it.[25] In the words of
another French radical:

> The defensive jihad doesn't need the *fatwa* as it is a personal duty
> for every individual. It is a method of protecting against injus-
> tices ... If an ordinary mortal commits an aggression against you
> without reason, in that case you are in self-defence ... Why did
> the French resist German occupation? Resistance is a legitimate
> right. Every people agrees with this logic. Religion, the laws,
> international law, they all guarantee this. It is an acquired right
> which doesn't need a legal frame.[26]

Based on this reasoning, therefore, there is an unequivocal case for
responding to attacks against the *umma*, which needs no formal or external
authorisation.

What, then, should this response consist of? The question of exactly
what 'defensive jihad' entails and how far one can go in exercising one's
duty is the subject of considerable debate amongst Islamist militants. The
'soft' militants, for example, believe that, even where gross violations of
the *umma* have taken place, certain 'laws of war' need to be respected. As

one British radical explained, there are clear distinctions between 'jihad' and terrorism:

> I understand the acts of resistance in Afghanistan. They are freedom fighters. They didn't go to the United States to carry out acts of terrorism. I sympathise with the people who fight in Afghanistan, in Iraq, in Palestine, in Sudan. I don't agree with the ones who commit acts in an underground, a train, a plane. The true *Mujahideen* are those who fight against American terrorism and the Zionists ... What some are doing in Muslim countries and what others are doing in Europe, it's not the same thing. The Taliban retaliate against an external enemy ... In Islam, it is all very clear: one does not kill the elderly, women, and boys.[27]

'Hard' militants, on the other hand, have a more liberal interpretation of what kinds of actions are justified in 'jihad' and why. In their view, anyone who can somehow be held responsible for the plight of the *umma* may be punished as an enemy of Islam. Taken to its logical conclusion, this seems to entail a form of collective responsibility shared by the civilian populations of democratic nations whose governments are believed to be part of the 'Crusader and Zionist Coalition'. In the words of a French radical:

> Every individual has his share of responsibility in what is currently going on in the world. Who elected the president of the United States? The American people. Why did they vote for Bush? They elected him for a political programme, and they were aware of his policy. You can't tell me the American people are innocent! If the American state invaded Iraq, then the people bear the entire responsibility because they chose this programme.[28]

In essence, this argument – which is a constant theme among Western Islamist militants – uses democracy as a means whereby entire populations can be made legitimate targets for violent 'jihad'. This logic was applied by Khan's protégé, Shehzad Tanweer, in his suicide video when he explained that 'you [the British people] are those who have voted in your government who in turn have and still to this day continues [sic] to oppress our mothers and children'.[29] Khan put it even more aggressively: 'Until you stop the bombing, gassing, imprisonment and torture of my people, we will not stop this fight ... Now you too will taste the reality of this situation.'[30]

Table 4: **The process of message dissemination**

Cognitive openings	Frame alignment	Justification of violence
Based on...	Based on...	Based on...
• Alienation from Western society	• Religious commitment	• *Umma* as the new identity
• Alienation from 'cultural Islam'	• Separation from society	• Legitimacy of violent 'jihad'
•'Humiliation by proxy'	• Imperative of 'jihad'	• 'Liberal' interpretation of 'jihad'

However, it would be a mistake to assume that concepts and doctrines such as 'jihad' and 'kuffar' are always well thought through and articulated. Rather, it seems as if some members of the Islamist militant movement are using them as convenient tools with which to legitimise their frustrations and their hatred of the societies in which they live. This clearly seems to have been the case with the Hofstad group in the Netherlands, which tended to come up with grotesquely violent ideas for how to kill public figures *prior* to looking for ways in which such actions could be justified in theological terms.[31]

The same was true of the group of young British Muslims who were convicted of terrorist offences in April 2007. Some of their conversations, which had been secretly taped by the Security Service, were played in court. At one point, a member of the group told his comrades that all kinds of attacks against non-believers were justified because 'when we kill the kuffar, this is because we know Allah hates the kuffar'.[32] One of the key targets identified by the group was one of London's biggest nightclubs. The group's rationalisation for choosing the target is a perfect illustration of the degree to which religious doctrines had come to be a convenient cover for members' personal frustration, but also an indication of how isolated they had become from mainstream opinion. In their own words: 'No one can put their hands up and say they are innocent – those slags dancing around'.[33]

This chapter has shown how messages play a critical role in facilitating potential recruits' transition towards Islamist militancy (see Table 4). Frequent references have been made to various media that are being used – especially 'jihadist' video tapes – but little has been said about the new online environment in which radicalisation and recruitment are often said to take place. The role of the Internet in Islamist militant recruitment is the subject of the next chapter.

CHAPTER FIVE

The Internet

In the long term, no development is likely to be more profound in its impact on Western societies than the so-called information revolution, which has resulted in the unprecedented rise of the Internet since the mid 1990s. It is impossible to say how many websites there are, partly because the numbers are changing so quickly. A survey in August 2008 estimated that more than a million websites were being added every month.[1] The search engine Google had indexed one trillion web pages in July last year, but – according to its chief executive – it was capturing only a minuscule percentage of what is currently online.[2]

Violent extremists are using the Internet in very much the same way as everyone else.[3] They are taking advantage of the low cost of Internet-based communication; the unlimited access to much of the world's knowledge it provides; the ease with which it facilitates the creation of networks among like-minded individuals, even across great distances; and the degree of anonymity which permits users to engage in otherwise risky or embarrassing behaviour.[4]

All the real-world participants in the Islamist militant movement – the 'hard core' leadership of al-Qaeda, the radical imams, the 'strategic thinkers' and the grassroots movement – are represented on the Internet. They all contribute to an anarchic structure of not just static websites but interactive web forums and so-called distributor sites, which make it possible for users to get from one place to the next, download new videos, and find updated links where sites have been taken down or changed their location.[5] Indeed, one of the great difficulties for those wishing to combat Islamist militants activities is that none of the participants are purely passive recipients of information: to some extent, all the actors listed above – including the growing number of grassroots 'jihadists' – play some role in producing and disseminating information.[6]

It is perhaps no longer a surprise that this new medium has come to play an important role in the processes of radicalisation and recruitment. But what exactly is its function? There are two principal ways in which the Internet has come to be used in the process of joining the Islamist militant movement: 'Internet-supported recruitment' and 'self-recruitment'.

Internet-supported recruitment

Most experts reject the notion of Internet-led recruitment. According to Wiktorowicz, exceptionally 'risky' behaviours, such as engaging in violence or crime, always require social networks in order for the perceived cost–benefit calculation to tip in their favour. He argues that involvement in violence needs to be preceded by a prolonged process of 'socialisation' in which perceptions of self-interest diminish and the value of group loyalties and personal ties increases.[7] This corresponds with Sageman's argument that, 'for the type of allegiance that the jihad demands, there is no evidence that the Internet is persuasive enough by itself'.[8]

Indeed, none of the radicals interviewed had been recruited solely on the Internet. Nor did any of the community leaders or law-enforcement and intelligence officials believe that the online environment would ever completely replace personal interaction. A London imam summed it up as follows: 'Human contact is important because [recruitment] is all about who knows whom. One guy knows a friend who knows a friend, and so on.'[9] Rejection of the idea of Internet-led recruitment does not, however, exclude some role for the Internet. In fact, whilst pointing out that the Internet is far from replacing human interaction, all the interviewees stressed that it could play an important role in *supporting* the process of joining the movement.

Firstly, the Internet can be useful in illustrating and reinforcing ideological messages and narratives. Through the Internet, potential recruits can gain near-instantaneous access to visually powerful video and imagery which appear to substantiate extremists' claims. This is what seems to happen during private study sessions, especially in the period of frame alignment. According to a British security official, 'the recruiter will be able to point out Internet sites that illustrate the narrative, and which explain what he was talking about in the abstract'.[10] A similar observation was made by a Spanish official:

> After the first meeting, when they are gradually introduced to a more private and select environment, the Internet and other media are being used to hammer home religious and political messages to increase commitment and dedication. The Internet gives them religious and practical instructions [and] ideological guidance, but also friends and support.[11]

Arguably, it is the very act of participating in a 'jihadist' web forum that allows participants to experience the sensation of being part of a global movement. After all, the Internet both represents and powerfully projects the sense of *umma* – that is, being part of a global community of believers – on which the ideology of the Islamist militant movement rests.[12]

Secondly, the Internet makes it easier to join and integrate with more formal organisations. It provides a comparatively risk-free way for potential recruits to find like-minded individuals and network amongst them, enabling them to reach beyond an isolated core group of conspirators. Indeed, it may allow self-starter cells to identify 'links to the jihad' and, thus, become 'guided cells' with access to the resources and strategic direction of the wider movement. The so-called Glostrup network in Denmark, for example, had tried to seek out 'links to the jihad' around Copenhagen for several months, but failed to identify anyone who could provide a connection to al-Qaeda. Only the Internet made it possible for them to 'hook up' with more experienced militants in other parts of Europe.[13] In that sense, one might compare the Internet to a recruitment magnet, which allows 'seekers' to find connections into the network, except that – in contrast to, say, radical mosques or radical bookshops – the Internet represents a virtual place.

Thirdly, the Internet creates a new social environment in which otherwise unacceptable views and behaviour are normalised. Bringing together like-minded individuals, the Internet becomes a virtual 'echo chamber' in which the most extreme ideas and suggestions receive the most encouragement and support. A Spanish official noted:

> People egg each other on. They compare themselves to other activists. They realise that a lot more people are doing this than what it first seemed. Sometimes, there seems to be a competition for who can be the most radical.[14]

Much of this may be theatre – a competition between 'armchair jihadists'[15] – but it may equally create an environment of hyper-radicalisation in which – akin to the phenomenon of 'group-think'[16] – the most extreme ideas and suggestions receive the most encouragement and support.

There can be no doubt that the phenomenon of Internet-supported recruitment will grow in importance. Although the Internet has been widely used among Islamist militants since the late 1990s, the breakthrough only came with the Iraq war in 2003, which mobilised the movement to an unprecedented degree and happened at a time when broadband Internet connections had just become affordable.[17] As it has become more risky for Islamist militants to propagate their views in the real world, an obvious response has been to exploit the virtual environment. Indeed, there has been a steep rise in the number of web forums and sites available in modern European languages, reaching out especially to converts and second- and third-generation European Muslims.[18]

Self-recruitment

Despite most experts' rejection of the idea of Internet-led recruitment, it seems clear that, in recent years, new and almost entirely virtual forms of Islamist militant activism have emerged, which have an impact upon traditional patterns of recruitment. It may be too early to say whether these forms of activism (which, so far, are mostly known about through anecdotal evidence) constitute a trend, but – if sustained – they could challenge the hitherto dominant notion of how Internet-supported recruitment works.

Two examples may serve to illustrate the point. The first is the case of London-based Younis Tsouli, better known as 'irhabi007' ('terrorist007'), who emerged as the undisputed 'superstar' of the online 'jihadist' scene in early 2004. Tsouli had joined a number of popular web forums and forged a (virtual) relationship with the spokesman of Abu Musab al-Zarqawi, the (then) leader of al-Qaeda in Mesopotamia. Tsouli's help on a number of occasions in publishing and disseminating Zarqawi's statements gave him enormous credibility with the rest of the online 'jihadist' community. In addition, his background in computing enabled him to provide assistance for other web 'jihadists', who turned to him for advice on internet security, hacking websites, and other technical questions.[19] As a result, within a matter of months, Tsouli had become one of the key hubs in the world of 'jihadism online', receiving hundreds of emails and requests each day. In fact, he was in touch with several Islamist militant groups across Europe, North America and the Middle East, and is believed to have brokered 'links to the jihad' for several leaderless cells.[20]

After about a year of online activism, Tsouli seems to have concluded that he wanted to participate in a suicide attack. The British authorities, who arrested Tsouli in his flat in West London in early 2005, claim that he had decided to blow himself up in London during the Christmas period that year.[21] The story of Tsouli is compelling because not only had the 22-year-old progressed from being a nobody to being one of the movement's most prominent figures in less than a year, he had radicalised himself to the point where he decided to become a martyr in the real world. The key point here is that neither his online career nor his radicalisation had ever required him to leave the comfort of his home. They all took place virtually, with Tsouli acting as his own recruiter. According to journalist Yassin Musharbash, 'The case of "irhabi 007" proves that the boundaries between virtual and actual terrorism – between Internet jihad and real attacks – have become porous'.[22]

A less spectacular, though still noteworthy, case is that of Irfan Raja, a 19-year-old student from Ilford near London, who was indicted for downloading and sharing extremist materials in September 2007 along with four other British Muslims of Pakistani descent. Raja had no known associations with the Islamist militant movement in his hometown, nor did any of his friends, associates or relatives know that he was interested in radical Islam. As in Tsouli's case, Raja's entire radicalisation took place on the Internet. He probably spent hundreds of hours downloading videos, posting messages and chatting to others in web forums.[23]

One day, Raja announced his intention to join the jihad, and a radical imam (apparently based in the United States) facilitated a connection with four others, who had the same idea and were based in Bradford, around 350 kilometres from Raja's hometown. On one of the web forums, which all of them had often visited, they found a more experienced member of the movement, who gave them instruction on how to make their way to a training camp in Pakistan's North West Frontier Province. The plan came close to reality, but Raja's parents became so concerned about their son that they called the police after discovering what seemed like a suicide note which he had written shortly before setting off for Bradford and Pakistan.[24]

In both cases, rather than merely supporting the process, the Internet seems to have driven the individuals' radicalisation and recruitment. Two cases may not be sufficient to declare the dawn of a new era in which neither human contact nor geographical proximity are necessary in order for people to become members of the Islamist militant movement. They represent a small minority, no doubt, but it would be a mistake to brush aside or ignore these instances of self-recruitment merely because they do not fit with long-established views about group dynamics and the importance of social bonds. It is easy to forget how quickly the Internet has

evolved, and it may well be the case, therefore, that widely held assumptions will have to be reassessed as the new medium continues to change
the way in which we communicate.

CONCLUSION

This paper has presented an overview of the process through which individuals in Western Europe become involved in the Islamist militant movement. The conclusions can be summed up as follows.

In recent years, recruitment efforts have been driven underground. Little overt recruitment and propagation now occurs at mosques, as many recruitment magnets have been shut down. But prisons and other places of vulnerability continue to be a cause of concern.

Different kinds of actors facilitate the process of recruitment, though little evidence has been found of systematic top-down recruitment. Radical imams have lost influence, and activists have emerged as the real engines of (mostly low-level) Islamist militant recruitment, with gateway organisations frequently (and sometimes unwittingly) providing a pool of potential candidates.

In European countries with a second and third generation of Muslims, Islamist militants often attempt to exploit young Muslims' identity crises. If successful, such cognitive openings make way for more extensive processes of learning, which may culminate in the justification of violence.

The role of the Internet has become more significant. Its principal function is to support real-world recruitment, but new forms of Islamist militant online activism have emerged, which rely less on human contact and could be described as self-recruitment.

What can be done? In outlining policy recommendations, it makes sense to differentiate between short-term measures that are aimed at curbing recruitment, and long-term policies which aim to address the risk factors that underlie the process of mobilisation.

Disrupting recruitment

Short-term measures are meant to disrupt the process of recruitment but are unlikely to affect the underlying grievances and strains that drive recruitment.

Firstly, it is of vital importance to prevent the emergence of recruitment magnets that allow seekers and self-starters to find connections into the Islamist militant network ('links to the jihad') and, thus, gain access to the resources and strategic direction of al-Qaeda. The term 'recruitment magnet' refers to fixed physical locations (such as radical bookshops or radical mosques), but may also be used to describe radical imams or virtual locations. In moving against existing recruitment magnets, it will be important to consider the risk of turning radicals into martyrs, and action against them should therefore be accompanied by a communication strategy that clearly distinguishes between extremists and the vast majority of decent, law-abiding mainstream Muslims.

Secondly, European governments urgently need to address the situation in prisons, which have emerged as principal hubs for Islamist militant radicalisation and recruitment. There needs to be heavy investment in training and staff. A system of 'certified imams' may be difficult to implement, but – where this has been adopted as the official policy – it should be pursued with urgency and vigour. Many non-European countries have experimented with de-radicalisation programmes, and European governments should do their utmost to learn from their successes and mistakes.

Thirdly, the efforts of law-enforcement and intelligence agencies should be firmly focused on the activist leaders of cells. They are the drivers of Islamist militant recruitment – they 'make things happen', initiate low-level spotting, and often represent a link into the wider network. On the other hand, being active members of their communities, they are also the most visible members of a cell, which should make identification and tracking easier.

Fourthly, European governments need to find a more consistent approach towards gateway organisations. Organisations which sanction or incite violence, propagate anti-Semitism or, more generally, encourage hatred towards other religions must never be seen as allies in counter-radicalisation. Purely religious organisations, on the other hand, may act as facilitators in local grassroots counter-radicalisation programmes. Even so, governments should resist the temptation of portraying them as competent to speak on behalf of Muslim communities. In no European country do the Tabligh or Salafi groups represent the mainstream, nor can their rigid faith practices be considered helpful in promoting Muslims' integration into modern European democracies.

Fifthly, more attention needs to be paid to the Internet. Governments need to become as Internet-savvy as the extremists they mean to counter, which requires investment in staff and technical means. The Internet, of course, is difficult to regulate, and technical measures – such as the filtering and blocking of content – may be neither desirable nor effective in a liberal democratic environment. In exceptional cases, governments should reserve the right to take disruptive measures, but the main thrust of governments' policies in this arena should be directed towards monitoring and towards enabling mainstream communities to counter the extremists' arguments.

Addressing risk factors

The long-term measures that are listed in the following aim to address some of the grievances and strains that make extremist ideologies resonate and might therefore be exploited by Islamist militants in their recruitment. The effect of these measures will not be immediately obvious, but they are nevertheless critical in undermining the movement's potential support base.

Mainstream Muslim communities, especially where a second and third generation of European Muslims exist, need to be re-vitalised and empowered. Islamist militants exploit generational conflicts and skilfully capitalise on the lack of social capital in many of these communities. Mainstream community leaders need to be supported – sometimes with money, sometimes politically – in providing more effective mechanisms for local democracy and accountability, as well as leisure activities and educational opportunities for young people.

It is vitally important for law-enforcement agencies to know and be trusted by the communities they serve. Unfortunately, police are often seen as an instrument of repression by Muslim minority communities. In their communication with the public, governments need to make it clear that they are on the side of mainstream Muslims. This means that seemingly repressive actions need to be explained, and that – where possible – communities should be consulted in the process of policymaking. Long-term engagement strategies as well as the systematic consideration of community impact are strategies that could facilitate the building of trust. But police forces also need to make systematic efforts to recruit more ethnic-minority personnel.

Educational institutions, especially schools, need to play a prominent role in countering violent extremists' efforts to gain support and mobilise potential recruits. Schools need to be active in addressing the narratives of violent extremists, for example by providing platforms in which issues likely to be raised by violent extremists are discussed openly, questions and contradictions highlighted, and alternative courses of action pointed out.

The provision of appealing European-language web content that addresses young Muslims' issues and conflicts in modern European societies is a challenge in the short as well as the long term. The production of such content cannot be imposed through government initiatives alone, but governments can offer incentives and encouragement.

None of the measures outlined here – even if fully implemented – will make the Islamist militant movement go away. They may help in undermining its home-grown base of support and, thus, reduce the likelihood that atrocities such as the London or Madrid bombings will be repeated. Ultimately, though, recruitment is not just a security problem. The challenge for Europe lies in constructing more inclusive societies in which the narratives of exclusion and grievances will not resonate.

NOTES

Introduction

1 See 'The International Terrorist Threat to the UK', speech given by Dame Eliza Manningham Buller at Queen Mary's College, London, 9 November 2006, available at http://www.mi5.gov.uk/output/speeches-by-the-director-general.html.

2 'Intelligence, Counter-terrorism and Trust', speech given by Jonathan Evans at the Society of Editors' conference, Manchester, 5 November 2007, available at http://www.mi5.gov.uk/output/speeches-by-the-director-general.html.

3 See ICSR/King's College London, 'Recruitment and Mobilisation for the Islamist Militant Movement in Europe', a study commissioned by the Directorate General for Justice, Freedom and Security of the European Commission, October 2008, available at http://ec.europa.eu/justice_home/fsj/terrorism/prevention/fsj_terrorism_prevention_prevent_en.htm.

4 See Michael Taarnby, 'Jihad in Denmark: An Overview and Analysis of Jihadi Activity in Denmark, 1990–2006', *Danish Institute of International Affairs Working Paper*, 2006/35, p. 62.

5 Taarnby, 'Recruitment of Islamist Terrorists in Europe: Trends and Perspectives', research report funded by the Danish Ministry of Justice, 14 January 2005, p. 6.

6 See, for example, Clark McCauley, 'Mechanisms of Political Radicalization: Pathways Toward Terrorism', *Terrorism and Political Violence,* vol. 20, no. 3, 2008, pp. 415–33.

7 Some scholars emphasise a fourth 'ingredient' – a so-called 'tipping point' – which, they argue, is needed to explain individuals' progression from one stage to the next. I am grateful to Marc Sageman for this insight.

8 See AIVD, *Recruitment for the Jihad in the Netherlands* (The Hague: AIVD, 2002), p. 7.

9 Marc Sageman, *Understanding Terror Networks* (Philadelphia, PA: University of Pennsylvania Press, 2004), p. 122.

10 *Ibid.*

11 Fernando Reinares, quoted in David J. Kilcullen, 'Subversion and Countersubversion in the Campaign against Terrorism in Europe', *Studies in Conflict and Terrorism,* vol. 30, no. 8, 2007, p. 652.

12 Roger Scruton, *The Palgrave Macmillan Dictionary of Political Thought,* 3rd ed. (Basingstoke: Palgrave Macmillan, 2007).

13 Alex Schmid, 'Terrorism – The Definitional Problem', *Case Western Reserve Journal of International Law,* vol. 36, no. 2, 2004, p. 376. For a useful taxonomy of the concepts of terror and terrorism, see Preston King,

'Challenging Democratic Sovereignty', *Survival*, vol. 50, no. 2, April–May 2008.

14 Alex Schmid and Albert Jongman, *Political Terrorism* (New Brunswick, NJ: Transaction Books, 1988), pp. 5–6.

15 Report of the Secretary-General's High Level Panel, United Nations Document A/59/565 (2004). For the EU's technical definition, see European Union, *Council Framework Decision on Combating Terrorism*, 13 June 2002, EU Document 2002/475/JHA.

16 See, for example, John Esposito, *Unholy War: Terror in the Name of Islam* (Oxford: Oxford University Press, 2002); Gilles Kepel, *Jihad: Expansion et Déclin de l'Islamisme* (Paris: Éditions Gallimard, 2000); Guido Steinberg, *Der nahe und der ferne Feind* (Munich: C.H. Beck, 2005); Quintan Wiktorowicz, 'A Genealogy of Radical Islam', *Studies in Conflict and Terrorism*, vol. 28, no. 2, 2005, pp. 75–97.

17 Not all Salafis are militant Islamists. For distinctions amongst followers of the Salafi movement, see Quintan Wiktorowicz, 'Anatomy of the Salafi Movement', *Studies in Conflict and Terrorism*, vol. 29, no. 3, 2006, pp. 207–39.

18 See Esposito, *Unholy War: Terror in the Name of Islam*, pp. 26–8. The definition follows the typology put forward by David Kilcullen in 'Subversion and Countersubversion in the Campaign against Terrorism in Europe', p. 653.

19 See ICSR/King's, 'Recruitment and Mobilisation'.

20 See Ceri Peach, 'Muslim Population of Europe: A Brief Overview of Demographic Trends and Socioeconomic Integration', in Center for Strategic and International Studies, *Muslim Integration: Challenging Conventional Wisdom in Europe and the United States* (Washington, DC: CSIS, 2007), p. 9.

Chapter One

1 See, for example, Sean O'Neill, 'Al Qaeda Will Strike Again', *The Times*, 30 April 2007.

2 See, for example, Robert Leiken, 'Europe's Angry Muslims', *Foreign Affairs*, July/August 2005; Udo Ulfkotte, *Heiliger Krieg in Europa* (Frankfurt/Main: Eichborn, 2007) pp. 120–135; Tim Winter, 'Islamism and Europe's Muslims: Recent Trends', in CSIS, *Muslim Integration: Challenging Conventional Wisdom in Europe and the United States*, pp. 33–44.

3 See Peach, 'Muslim Population of Europe: A Brief Overview of Demographic Trends and Socioeconomic Integration', p. 9.

4 Olivier Roy, *Globalized Islam: The Search for a New Ummah* (New York: Columbia University Press, 2004), pp. 303–9. Also Peter R. Neumann, 'The Appeal of Jihad', *International Herald Tribune*, 5 July 2007.

5 Peach, 'Muslim Population of Europe: A Brief Overview of Demographic Trends

and Socioeconomic Integration', p. 13.

6 *Ibid.*, p. 12.

7 Taarnby, 'Recruitment of Islamist Terrorists in Europe: Trends and Perspectives', p. 36.

8 Confidential interview with British official, London, July 2007.

9 See Jytte Klausen, *The Islamic Challenge: Politics and Religion in Western Europe* (Oxford: Oxford University Press, 2005), pp. 157, 192, 220.

10 Of the approximately 1.6m British Muslims, about 750,000 are of Pakistani descent. The next largest countries of origin are Bangladesh (280,000) and India (130,000). In Germany, of the 3.5m Muslims residing in the country, nearly 2m are of Turkish descent, followed by Bosnia (160,000) and Morocco (73,000); see Peach, 'Muslim Population of Europe: A Brief Overview of Demographic Trends and Socioeconomic Integration', p. 11.

11 Foreign Office memo, quoted in 'Leaked Memo Shows Blair Told of Iraq War Terror Link', *Observer*, 28 August 2005.

12 'Few Signs of Backlash from Western Europeans', Pew Research Center, 6 July 2006, http://pewglobal.org/reports/pdf/254.pdf.

13 For the most authoritative account of al-Qaeda's foundation, see Lawrence Wright, *The Looming Tower: Al-Qaeda's Road to 9/11* (London: Penguin, 2006), esp. Chapter 6.

14 This refers to the so-called Bojinka plot in which Ramzi Yousef, who had been behind the first World Trade Center bombing in 1993, was hoping to bring down up to a dozen passenger planes in mid-flight. During a test run, one passenger on a flight from the Philippines to Tokyo was killed. See Oliver Schröm, *Al Qaida: Akteure, Strukturen, Attentate* (Frankfurt/Main: Links, 2003), Chapter 4.

15 'List of Al Qaida Inspired Terror Attacks Released', Prime Minister's Office, 13 July 2005, available at http://www.number-10.gov.uk/output/Page7930.asp.

16 Cited in Congressional Research Service, 'Terrorist Attacks by Al Qaeda', 31 March 2004. Former President Bill Clinton strongly denies that 'Black Hawk Down' had anything to do with al-Qaeda. In a recent television interview, he claimed that 'no living soul' believed that this was the work of Osama bin Laden and his organisation. See 'Transcript: William Jefferson Clinton on "Fox News Sunday"', 26 September 2006; available at http://www.foxnews.com/story/0,2933,215397,00.html.

17 See Paul L. Williams, *Al Qaeda: Brotherhood of Terror* (New York: Alpha, 2002), Chapters 7 and 8. Also Rohan Gunaratna, *Inside Al Qaeda* (London: Hurst, 2002), esp. Chapter 2.

18 See Olivier Roy, 'Netzwerk des Terrors – Markenzeichen al-Qaida', *Le Monde Diplomatique* (German edition), 10 September 2004; Peter Bergen, *Holy War Inc: Inside the Secret World of Osama bin Laden* (London: Phoenix, 2001), Chapter 10.

19 Bruce Hoffman, 'The Changing Face of Al Qaeda and the Global War on Terrorism', *Studies in Conflict and Terrorism*, vol. 27, no. 6, 2004, pp. 549–560. Also Jessica Stern, 'The Protean Enemy', *Foreign Affairs*, July/August 2003, pp. 27–40.

20 See Jason Burke, *Al Qaeda: The True Story of Radical Islam* (London: I.B. Tauris, 2003).

21 Cited in Brynjar Lia, 'The al-Qaida Strategist Abu Mus'ab al-Suri: A Profile', OMS-Seminar Presentation, Oslo, 15 March 2006, p. 17, available at http://www.mil.no/multimedia/archive/00076/_The_Al-Qaida_strate_76568a.pdf.

22 *ibid*.

23 See, for example, Robert S. Leiken, 'Europe's Angry Muslims'.

24 The term was coined by Daniel Benjamin and Steven Simon. See Dan Benjamin and Steven Simon, *The Next Attack* (New York: Henry Holt, 2005), pp. 27–31. Also Aidan Kirby, 'The London Bombers as "Self-Starters": A Case Study in Indigenous Radicalization and the Emergence of Autonomous Cliques', *Studies in Conflict and Terrorism*, vol. 30, no. 5, 2007, pp. 415–28.

25 See Sageman, *Understanding Terror Networks*, Chapter 4.

26 See, for example, Lorenzo Vidino, 'The Hofstad Group: The New Face of Terrorist Networks in Europe', *Studies in Conflict and Terrorism*, vol. 30, no. 7, 2007, pp. 579–92. Also Yassin Musharbash, *Die neue Al-Qaida* (Cologne: Kiepenheuer und Witsch, 2006), pp. 245–51.

27 Marc Sageman, *Leaderless Jihad: Terror Networks in the Twenty-First Century* (Philadelphia, PA: University of Pennsylvania Press, 2008), p. 144.

28 See Javier Jordán, 'Mapping Jihadist Terrorism in Spain', *Studies in Conflict and Terrorism*, vol. 28, no. 2, 2005, pp. 169–91; and Lorenzo Vidino, *Al Qaeda in Europe* (Amherst, NY: Prometheus, 2006), Chapter 11.

29 See Shiraz Maher, 'Glasgow Bombs: The Doctor I Knew', *New Statesman*, 5 July 2007. Recently, there was

some speculation that some of the attackers were linked to al-Qaeda in Mesopotamia. See Raymond Bonner, Jane Perlez and Eric Schmitt, 'British Inquiry of Failed Plots Points to Iraq's Qaeda Group', *New York Times,* 14 December 2007.

30 See Vidino, 'The Hofstad Group: The New Face of Terrorist Networks in Europe'; Petter Nesser, 'Jihadism in Western Europe after the Invasion of Iraq: Tracing Motivational Influences from the Iraq War on Jihadist Terrorism in Western Europe', *Studies in Conflict and Terrorism,* vol. 29, no. 4, 2006, p. 336.

31 Sageman, *Leaderless Jihad: Terror Networks in the Twenty-First Century,* p. 144.

32 Bruce Hoffman, 'The Myth of Grass-Roots Terrorism: Why Osama bin Laden Still Matters', *Foreign Affairs,* May/June 2008, pp. 133–138.

33 *Ibid.*

34 Sageman, *Understanding Terror Networks,* p. 160.

35 Confidential interview with Spanish official, London, September 2007.

Chapter Two

1 AIVD, *Recruitment for the Jihad in the Netherlands,* p. 13.

2 During Abu Hamza's reign, for example, Finsbury Park attracted an audience of hundreds of Muslims from all over the United Kingdom, with many keen to sign up to violent jihad as soon as they had found their way to the building. See Sean O'Neill and Daniel McGrory, *The Suicide Factory: Abu Hamza and the Finsbury Park Mosque* (London: Harper, 2006), pp. 115–16.

3 Quintan Wiktorowicz, 'Joining the Cause: Al Muhajiroun and Radical Islam', unpublished paper, p. 8, available at http://www.yale-university.com/polisci/info/conferences/Islamic%20Radicalism/papers/wiktorowicz-paper.pdf.

4 Confidential interview with British community leader, London, July 2007.

5 *Ibid.*

6 *Ibid.*

7 Confidential interview with Spanish radical, Madrid, April 2007.

8 Confidential interview with French radical by Luiz Martinez, Paris, March 2007.

9 See 'Irak: trios Français présumés islamistes détenus par les Etats-Unis', *Le Monde,* 4 February 2005.

10 Vidino, 'Al Qaeda in Europe', pp. 271–4.

11 'A la mosque Adda'wa, à Paris: "On ne prêche pas le djihad ici"', *Le Monde,* 9 February 2005.

12 Confidential interview with British community leader, London, August 2007.

13 Confidential interview with Spanish official, London, September 2007.

14 See Pascale Combelles Siegel, 'An Inside Look at France's Mosque Surveillance Program', *Jamestown Terrorism Monitor,* 16 August 2007.

15 See, for example, James A. Beckford, Daniele Joly and Farhad Khosrokhavar, *Muslims in Prison: Challenges and Change in Britain and France* (Basingstoke: Palgrave, 2005); Jean-Luc Marret (ed.), *Les fabriques du jihad* (Paris: Presses Universitaires de France, 2005).

16 Olivier Roy, 'Terrorism and Deculturation', in Louise Richardson (ed.), *The Roots of Terrorism* (New York: Routledge, 2006), p. 162.

17 Confidential interview with British official by Brooke Rogers, Leeds, September 2007.

18 James Beckford, cited in 'Islamic Radcalization in Europe's Jails?', MSNBC.com, 8 July 2006.

19 Khosrokhavar, cited in Craig S. Smith, 'French Prisons – Radicalizing Large Muslim Populations', *New York Times,* 20 December 2004.

[20] Confidential interview with British official, London, August 2007; confidential interview with French official, Paris, September 2007.

[21] For example, in the wake of the 11 September 2001 attacks, a number of prison imams were suspended for 'unprofessional behaviour' in the UK after it emerged that they had been spreading the message of the radical cleric Abu Hamza. This included the prison imams at Feltham Young Offenders Institution, where Richard Reid – the so-called 'shoe bomber' – had been radicalised. See, for example, Alan Travis and Audrey Gillan, 'Bomb Suspect Became a Militant in Prison', *Guardian*, 28 July 2005.

[22] Confidential interview with Spanish official, London, September 2007.

[23] Dominique Gaulme, 'Islam en prison: missions d'urgence pour aumôniers musulmans', *Le Figaro*, 12 January 2007.

[24] Confidential interview with Spanish official, London, September 2007; confidential interview with British official, London, July 2007.

[25] Cited in Vidino, 'The Hofstad Group: The New Face of Terrorist Networks in Europe', p. 588.

[26] Confidential interview with British official, London, August 2007.

[27] For a snapshot of the situation in Spain, see '139 islamistas en las cárceles', *El País*, 28 October 2007. For a summary of an internal report of the Spanish Director General of Prisons, see 'Prisiones estima que el 50% de los musulanes…', *El Confidencial*, 30 June 2005.

[28] Fernando Reinares, 'Prisons and Radicalisation', paper delivered at 'Youth Radicalisation' workshop organised by the Global Institute for Counterterrorism, Rome, 11 July 2007.

[29] AIVD, *Recruitment for the Jihad in the Netherlands*, p. 14

[30] Serge F. Kovaleski and Alan Cowell, 'British Identify Two Principal Suspects', *New York Times*, 8 July 2007.

[31] See, for example, Anthony Glees and Chris Pope, *When Students Turn to Terror* (London: The Social Affairs Unit, 2005); Fidel Sendagorta, 'Jihad in Europe: The Wider Context', *Survival*, vol. 47, no. 3, 2005, p. 67; Michael Whine, 'Islamist Recruitment and Antisemitism on British Campuses', RUSI Workshop on Education and Extremism, 23 January 2006, paper available at http://www.thecst.org.uk/docs/RUSI%20Homeland%20Security.doc.

[32] Baber Siddiqi interviewed on BBC Radio 4, quoted in Glees and Pope, *When Students Turn to Terror*, p. 25.

Chapter Three

[1] Sageman, *Understanding Terror Networks*, p. 122.

[2] *Ibid.*

[3] A similar concept is that of the 'conveyor belt', which is meant to illustrate the continuum between non-violent forms of Islamist activism and Islamist militancy. See Zeyno Baran, 'Fighting the War of Ideas', *Foreign Affairs*, November/December 2005, pp. 68–78.

[4] Gilles Kepel, *The War for Muslim Minds: Islam and the West* (Cambridge, MA: Harvard University Press, 2004), p. 261.

[5] *Ibid.*, pp. 261–2.

[6] Klausen, *The Islamic Challenge: Politics and Religion in Western Europe*, p. 44.

[7] Omar Nasiri, *Mein Leben bei al-Qaida: Die Geschichte eines Spions* (Munich: DVA, 2006), p. 162.

[8] Javier Jordán, 'The Madrid Attacks: Results of Investigations Two Years Later', *Jamestown Terrorism Monitor*, 9 March 2006.

[9] See Shane Drennan and Andrew Black, 'Jihad Online – The Changing Role of the Internet', *Jane's Intelligence Review*, 19 July 2007.

68 | Peter R. Neumann

10 For an overview of HT ideology, see Jean-Francois Mayer, 'Hizb-ut Tahrir – The Next Al-Qaida, Really?', PSIO Occasional Paper, 4/2004. Also Ed Hussain, *The Islamist* (London: Penguin, 2007), esp. Chapters 6 and 7.

11 Mayer, 'Hizb-ut Tahrir – The Next Al-Qaida, Really?', pp. 16–17.

12 Jorgen Nielsen, *Muslims in Western Europe*, 3rd ed. (Edinburgh: Edinburgh University Press, 2004), p. 168.

13 Interview with Shiv Malik, London, July 2007. Also Shiv Malik, 'The New Terror', *New Statesman*, 5 July 2007.

14 Confidential interview with British official, London, August 2007; confidential interview with British radical, London, September 2007.

15 Michael Whine, 'Will the Ban on the Al Muhajiroun Successor Groups Work?', paper published by the International Institute for Counter-terrorism, 8 August 2006, available at http://www.ict.org.il/Articles/tabid/66/Articlsid/224/currentpage/7/Default.aspx

16 Ibid.

17 Taarnby, 'Jihad in Denmark: An Overview and Analysis of Jihadi Activity in Denmark, 1990–2006', p. 55.

18 Whine, 'Will the Ban on the Al Muhajiroun Successor Groups Work?'

19 See Zeyno Baran, 'Countering Ideological Support for Terrorism in Europe: Muslim Brotherhood and Hizb ut-Tahrir – Allies or Enemies?', *Connections*, vol. 5, no. 3, 2006, pp. 19–34; also Sendagorta, 'Jihad in Europe: The Wider Context', p. 67–9.

20 'The Evolution of Leadership in Europe's Global Jihad Networks', *Exclusive Analysis Report*, 21 September 2007, p. 13.

21 'Abdul-Jabbar van de Ven: Jongerenimam', *De Telegraaf*, 24 November 2004.

22 See AIVD, *Violent Jihad in the Netherlands: Current Trends in the Islamist Terrorist Threat* (The Hague: AIVD, 2006), p. 26.

23 The transcripts are available at http://dutchreport.blogspot.com/2005/01/chatting-with-terrorists.html.

24 Confidential interview with Spanish official, Madrid, August 2007; confidential interview with Spanish community leader, Madrid, September 2007.

25 Confidential interview with British community leader, London, August 2007; confidential interview with French community leader, Paris, September 2007.

26 Confidential interview with British official, London, July 2007; also interview with Shiv Malik, London, July 2007.

27 'Red Ameuroud a été expulse vers l'Algérie', Associated Press, 30 July 2005; for the controversial case of Abdelkader Bouziane, see Craig S. Smith, 'France Struggles to Curb Extremist Muslim Clerics', *New York Times*, 30 April 2004; also Keppel, *The War for Muslim Minds: Islam and the West*, pp. 258–60.

28 Confidential interview with French community leader, Paris, May 2007.

29 Confidential interview with French official, Paris, September 2007. Also Jon Henley, 'Muslims Are Not Cockroaches', *Guardian*, 11 August 2005.

30 Petter Nesser, 'Structures of Jihadist Terrorist Cells in the UK and Europe', paper given at the joint FFI/King's College London conference, 'The Changing Faces of Jihadism', London, 28 April 2006, available at http://www.mil.no/felles/ffi/start/FFI-prosjekter/Alfover/_TERRA/Publikasjoner/Speeches/.

31 'The Evolution of Leadership in Europe's Global Jihad Networks', p. 8

32 Nesser, 'Structures of Jihadist Terrorist Cells in the UK and Europe'.

33 Ibid.

34 For profiles of the three individuals mentioned here, see Vidino, 'The Hofstad Group: The New Face of Terrorist Networks in Europe'; Shiv Malik, 'My Brother the Bomber', *Prospect*, June 2007; Juzgado Central de Instrucción Número 6, *Audiencia Nacional*, Sumario No. 20/2004, 10 April 2006, pp. 1212–13.

35 See Javier Jordán, 'The Threat of Grassroots Jihadi Networks', *Jamestown Terrorism Monitor*, 15 February 2007, pp. 1–3.

36 Ibid.

[37] Sageman, *Understanding Terror Networks*, Chapter 3. Della Porta investigated members of Marxist terrorist groups in Italy and West Germany, concluding that 'the decision to join an underground organisation was rarely an individual one. For most of the militants, it involved cliques of friends.' See Donatella della Porta, *Social Movements, Political Violence and the State: A Comparative Analyis of Italy and Germany* (Cambridge: Cambridge University Press, 1995), p. 167.

[38] Edwin Bakker, 'Jihadi Terrorists in Europe', Clingendael Security Paper No. 2, Netherlands Institute of International Relations, December 2006, p. 56.

[39] I wish to thank Brooke Rogers for this insight. For the role of group dynamics more generally, see Jerrold M. Post, 'Terrorist Psycho-logic: Terrorist Behaviour as a Product of Psychological Forces', in Walter Reich (ed.), *Origins of Terrorism: Psychologies, Ideologies, Theologies, States of Mind* (Baltimore, MD: Johns Hopkins University Press, 1998), pp. 25–40; Brooke M. Rogers *et al.*, 'The Role of Religious Fundamentalism in Terrorist Violence: A Social Psychological Analysis', *The International Review of Psychiatry*, vol. 19, no. 3, 2007, p. 257.

[40] Confidential interview with Spanish official, London, September 2007.

[41] Confidential interview with French community leader, Paris, April 2007.

[42] See, for example, Della Porta, *Social Movements, Political Violence and the State*, p. 167; Farhad Khosrokhavar, *Les Nouveaux Martyrs d'Allah* (Paris: Flammarion, 2002), pp. 156, 167; Sageman, *Understanding Terror Networks*, pp. 126–30; Wiktorowicz, 'Joining the Cause: Al Muhajiroun and Radical Islam', p. 8.

[43] Interview with Shiv Malik, London, July 2007.

[44] Confidential interview with French community leader, Paris, May 2007; confidential interview with British community leader, London, July 2007.

Chapter Four

[1] Wiktorowicz, 'A Genealogy of Radical Islam'. For various excellent reports on Islamist militant ideology issues by the Combating Terrorism Centre at West Point, see http://ctc.usma.edu/publications/publications.asp.

[2] Andrew Silke, 'The Role of the Organisation in Suicide Terrorism', Proceedings of the British Psychological Society Seminar Series: Aspects of Terrorism and Martyrdom, published in the *International Journal of Mental Health and Addiction*, April 2006, available at http://www.ijma-journal.com/issues/conferences/abstracts/3.

[3] Harvey W. Kushner, 'Suicide Bombers: Business as Usual', *Studies in Conflict and Terrorism*, vol. 19, no. 4, 2006, pp. 329–37.

[4] Wiktorowicz, 'Joining the Cause: Al Muhajiroun and Radical Islam', p. 7.

[5] *Ibid.*, p. 8.

[6] Confidential interview with French radical by Luiz Martinez, Paris, March 2007.

[7] Confidential interview with French radical by Luiz Martinez, Paris, May 2007.

[8] Bakri, interviewed in June 2002, quoted in Wiktorowicz, 'Joining the Cause: Al Muhajiroun and Radical Islam', p. 16.

[9] *Ibid.*

[10] Interview with Shiv Malik, London, July 2007.

[11] *Ibid.*

[12] Sageman, *Leaderless Jihad: Terror Networks in the Twenty-First Century*, p. 72.

[13] Farhad Khosrokhavar, *Les Nouveaux Martyrs d'Allah* (Paris: Flammarion, 2002), p. 152.

[14] Confidential interview with French official, Paris, July 2007; confidential

interview with British official, London, August 2007.

15 See Robert D. Benford and David A. Snow, 'Framing Processes and Social Movements: An Overview and Assessment', *Annual Review of Sociology*, vol. 26, 2000, pp. 611–39. Also Wiktorowicz, 'Joining the Cause: Al Muhajiroun and Radical Islam', pp. 8–10.

16 Confidential interview with Spanish radical, Madrid, October 2007.

17 See, for example, Esposito, *Unholy War: Terror in the Name of Islam,* pp. 64–70.

18 Qatada, quoted in Juzgado Central de Instrucción Número 6, *Audiencia Nacional, Sumario No. 20/2004,* 10 April 2006, p. 1217. I wish to thank Rogelio Alonso for this reference and insight.

19 Wiktorowicz, 'Joining the Cause: Al Muhajiroun and Radical Islam', p. 5.

20 Steinberg, *Der nahe und der ferne Feind,* Chapter 2.

21 Confidential interview with British community leader, London, August 2007.

22 Jabbar, quoted in 'Abdul-Jabbar van de Ven: Jongerenimam', *De Telegraaf,* 24 November 2004.

23 Confidential interview with French radical by Luiz Martinez, Paris, April 2007.

24 *Ibid.*

25 Needless to say, what this paper refers to are jihadist doctrines, which – in most conventional scholars' view – completely contradict the Koran's stipulations about the laws of war and peace. See, for example, Shaheen Sardar Ali and Javaid Rehman, 'The Concept of *Jihad* in Islamic International Law', *Journal of Conflict and Security Law,* vol. 1, no. 1, 2005, pp. 1–23.

26 Confidential interview with French radical by Luiz Martinez, Paris, May 2007.

27 Confidential interview with Spanish radical, Madrid, September 2007.

28 Confidential interview with French radical by Luiz Martinez, Paris, May 2007.

29 'Video of 7 July Bomber Released', BBC News, 6 July 2006, available at http://news.bbc.co.uk/1/hi/uk/5154714.stm.

30 'London Bomber: Text in Full', BBC News, 1 September 2005, available at http://news.bbc.co.uk/1/hi/uk/4206800.stm.

31 See Vidino, 'The Hofstad Group: The New Face of Terrorist Networks in Europe'.

32 Quoted in Rosie Cowan, 'British Suspects Considered Blowing Up London Club, Court Told', *Guardian,* 23 March 2006.

33 *Ibid.*

Chapter Five

1 Netcraft, *Web Server Survey,* August 2008, available at http://news.netcraft.com/archives/2008/08/29/august_2008_web_server_survey.html.

2 See 'We Knew the Web Was Big', Google blog posting, available at http://googleblog.blogspot.com/2008/07/we-knew-web-was-big.html.

3 Timothy L. Thomas, 'Al Qaida and the Internet: The Danger of Cyberplanning', *Parameters,* vol. 33, no. 2, 2003, pp. 112–23. Also Gabriel Weimann, *Terror on the Internet: The New Arena, the New Challenges* (Washington DC: US Institute of Peace, 2006). A review of jihadism on the Internet was recently published by the Dutch National Coordinator Counterterrorism. See National Coordinator for Counterterrorism, *Jihadis and the Internet* (NCTb: The Hague, 2007), available at http://www.fas.org/irp/world/netherlands/jihadis.pdf.

4 I am grateful to Tim Stevens of the International Centre for the Study of Radicalisation and Political Violence (ICSR) for these insights.

5 Brynjar Lia, 'Al-Qaeda Online: Understanding Jihadist Internet

Infrastructure', *Jane's Intelligence Review*, 1 January 2006, pp. 2–5.

6 Hanna Rogan, 'Jihadism Online: A Study of How al-Qaida and Radical Islamist Groups Use the Internet for Terrorist Purposes', *FFI Report*, 2006/0915, p. 15.

7 Wiktorowicz, 'Joining the Cause: Al Muhajiroun and Radical Islam', pp. 8–10.

8 Sageman, *Understanding Terror Networks*, p. 163.

9 Confidential interview with British community leader, London, August 2007.

10 Confidential interview with British official, London, September 2007.

11 Confidential interview with Spanish official, London, September 2007. Similar findings were made as early as 2002 by the Dutch domestic intelligence service; see AIVD, *Recruitment for the Jihad in the Netherlands*, p. 15.

12 Sageman, *Understanding Terror Networks*, p. 161.

13 Taarnby, 'Jihad in Denmark: An Overview and Analysis of Jihadi Activity in Denmark, 1990–2006', pp. 44–7.

14 Confidential interview with Spanish official, London, September 2007.

15 Rogan, 'Jihadism Online: A Study of How al-Qaida and Radical Islamist Groups Use the Internet for Terrorist Purposes', p. 20.

16 See Irving Janis, *Groupthink: Psychological Studies of Policy Decisions and Fiascos*, 2nd ed. (Boston, MA: Houghton Mifflin, 1982).

17 See Hanna Rogan, 'Abu Reuter and the E-Jihad', *Georgetown Journal of International Affairs*, Summer 2007, pp. 89–96.

18 Lia, 'Al-Qaeda Online: Understanding Jihadist Internet Infrastructure'.

19 Site Institute, 'Irhabi 007 Unveiled: A Portrait of a Cyber-Terrorist', *Site Report*, 2006.

20 Yassin Musharbash, '37.000 Kreditkarten für "Terrorist 007"', *Spiegel Online*, 26 July 2007, available at http://www.spiegel.de/politik/ausland/0,1518,495468,00.html.

21 Musharbash, *Die neue Al-Qaida*, p. 155.

22 *Ibid.*

23 Dominic Casciani, 'Students Who Descended into Extremism', BBC News, 3 September 2007.

24 The note said: 'If not in this [world], we will meet in the [highest reaches of heaven'. See *ibid*.

The Evolution of Strategic Thought
Classic Adelphi Papers

The Adelphi Papers monograph series is the Institute's principal contribution to policy-relevant, original academic research. Collected on the occasion of the Institute's 50th anniversary, the twelve Adelphi Papers in this volume represent some of the finest examples of writing on strategic issues. They offer insights into the changing security landscape of the past half-century and glimpses of some of the most significant security events and trends of our times, from the Cold War nuclear arms race, through the oil crisis of 1973, to the contemporary challenge of asymmetric war in Iraq and Afghanistan.

Published April 2008; 704 pp.

CONTENTS:

Introduction
Patrick M. Cronin

The Evolution of NATO
Adelphi Paper 1, 1961
Alastair Buchan

Controlled Response and Strategic Warfare
Adelphi Paper 19, 1965
T. C. Schelling

The Control of Proliferation: Three Views
Adelphi Paper 29, 1966
Solly Zuckerman, Alva Myrdal and Lester B. Pearson

Israel and the Arab World: The Crisis of 1967
Adelphi Paper 41, 1967
Michael Howard and Robert Hunter

The Asian Balance of Power: A Comparison with European Precedents
Adelphi Paper 44, 1968
Coral Bell

Change and Security in Europe: Part II: In Search of a System
Adelphi Paper 49, 1968
Pierre Hassner

Urban Guerrilla Warfare
Adelphi Paper 79, 1971
Robert Moss

Oil and Influence: The Oil Weapon Examined
Adelphi Paper 117, 1975
Hanns Maull

The Spread of Nuclear Weapons: More May Be Better
Adelphi Paper 171, 1981
Kenneth N. Waltz

Intervention and Regional Security
Adelphi Paper 196, 1985
Neil Macfarlane

Humanitarian Action in War: Aid, Protection and Impartiality in a Policy Vacuum
Adelphi Paper 305, 1996
Adam Roberts

The Transformation of Strategic Affairs
Adelphi Paper 379, 2006
Lawrence Freedman

Bookpoint Ltd. 130 Milton Park, Abingdon, Oxon OX14 4SB, UK
Tel: +44 (0)1235 400524, Fax: +44 (0)1235 400525
Customer orders: book.orders@tandf.co.uk
Bookshops, wholesalers and agents:
Email (UK): uktrade@tandf.co.uk,
email (international): international@tandf.co.uk

Routledge
Taylor & Francis Group

THE INTERNATIONAL INSTITUTE FOR STRATEGIC STUDIES